SCHOOL BEHAVIOR AND SCHOOL DISCIPLINE

Coping with Deviant Behavior in the Schools

Eve E. Gagné
Chicago State University

UNIVERSITY
PRESS OF
AMERICA

Copyright © 1982 by

University Press of America, Inc.

P.O. Box 19101, Washington, D.C. 20036

Library of Congress Cataloging in Publication Data

Gagne, Eve E.
    School behavior and school discipline.

    Includes index.
    1. School discipline. 2. Deviant behavior.
I. Title.
LB3012.G33 1982   371.5   82-15912
ISBN 0-8191-2748-5
ISBN 0-8191-2749-3 (pbk.)

To my Mom and Dad

With Love and Gratitude

ACKNOWLEDGEMENTS

Every teacher is ultimately a student; in seventeen years as an educator, I learned a great deal from the children and adults who have been my students. Unfortunately, it is impossible to acknowledge every student who has influenced the development of my attitudes towards school behavior and school discipline; consequently, many of the students to whom I have acquired a debt of gratitude are not included. This text would not have been possible without the encouragement and support of many students. Ideas for this book were first developed at the State University of New York at Binghamton; I would also like to thank the students, faculty, and staff at Chicago State University, who have been very supportive during the development of this book. Thanks are due to Doug Michaud, and to Ted Michaud, for the insight they have given me regarding the joys and sorrows of growing up.

I have been greatly influenced by my work at the University of Connecticut, and Dr. A. J. Pappanikou's ideas on mental health in the schools have been a major building block in my construction of a child advocate model for school discipline. I would also like to thank Sue Bennett, Jacquetta Carr, Artie Carter, Margaret Goodman, Carmen Guillard, Jean Jones, Ellen Kaufman, Steve Marcus, Muriel Rossi, Sandra Rance, Marge Ryan, Marvie Sparks, and Renee Mitchell, for their interest, support, and insight. Special thanks are due to David Masters, whose inspiration has encouraged me in my pursuit of knowledge, particularly in the area of deviant behavior and human rights. I also owe a debt of gratitude to Anita Tutson, who has been instrumental in the development of several important concepts included in Chapters Four and Five, particularly the concept of communion. Dean Barbara Kardas has been instrumental in the author's conceptualization and understanding of the holistic acceptance of others.

The expert help of Marni Gagne has been indispensable in the editing and production of the manuscript in its final form; her personal support also made completion of this book possible.

Despite the help that the author received from published and unpublished sources, any errors of fact, or of omission, are the author's own, as is always the case in published works.

CONTENTS

Preface

Too often, school discipline is interpreted as a punitive procedure and appropriate school behavior is interpreted as conforming behavior. This book examines school discipline from an inter-disciplinary framework which includes the fields of education, sociology, psychology, philosophy, and law. Despite the fact that Gallup polls indicate that the general public, as well as professional educators, see discipline as the most important problem facing the schools, surprisingly few books have been published in the field of school discipline. When books are written on school discipline, they are often of the cookbook variety. It is difficult to imagine a legitimate cookbook in the complex area of school discipline; such books can do no more than help teachers become behavioral technicians. Certainly, behavior management is important, but more important than the management of behavior is the determination of which behaviors should be encouraged, which behaviors should be discouraged, and which behaviors should simply be tolerated. The present book does present some technical guidelines in the area of behavior management, but, more importantly, it examines school behavior from a global perspective. Rather than being a cookbook, the present text is a travel guide which takes the reader into uncharted areas in the field of school discipline. The relativity of behavior and the individuality of the student is stressed, as is the fact that deviant behavior is often highly desirable. School discipline is examined as it is and as it could be.

Chapter One

AN INTRODUCTION TO DEVIANCE

The Schools

School discipline problems are recognized as a major issue by almost everyone. Students often see themselves as victims in a ruthless society of pranksters, gangsters and vice principals. Teachers see themselves as unwilling prison guards who must contend with violence, vandalism and classroom clownery. The day before the beginning of the school year may soon become a national holiday named "Detention Slip Day", this is the day that thousands of teachers rush to their principals's offices for an arsenal of detention slips.

The word is out. Children have rights! Girls can fight! Sex, alcohol and pot are great. Kid power has flourished and school authority has diminished. Somewhere in the hot summers of the 1960's big people and little people, older people and younger people were made equal. Horatio Alger books once taught children that hard work and honesty was the right way to success, but television coverage of Watergate, the CIA and the FBI taught the children that dishonesty may be more successful than honesty, and hardwork may not be relevant. Children now live in a dustbowl where simple blacks and whites have changed into shades of grey.

Social conditions have changed, students have changed, teachers have changed, but the school authority structure has not changed. Schools are ultimately controlled by lay boards of education which often believe school in the 1980's should be as school was in the 1950's. Schools are still buildings rather than learning programs and self-contained classrooms are still the basic building block of the school. The "back to basics" movement ironically means that children are to be taught more reading, writing and arithmetic as if these subjects are more "basic" than is getting along with others in a world which seems ready to self-destruct.

School Behavior Problems As Deviance

As will be seen, if school behavior problems did not exist, they would have to be invented. School behavior problems will be treated as "deviance" in this book. "Deviant behavior" will be defined as the conduct of a person in a given social role which does not conform to the expectations of the reference group. Everyone fills numerous social roles; thus, one may simultaneously be a son, a student, a teenager, and a gang member. One's primary reference group varies with varying roles. Thus, one's primary reference group would be one's peers; as a student, the primary reference group would be school personnel. Young children have fewer reference groups than older children. Parents and teachers are the primary reference groups for young children; that is, young children define the appropriateness or inappropriateness of their behaviors according to the expectations of their parents and teachers. Adolescents have a wide variety of reference groups, a very important one being the peer reference group. The greater the number of reference groups, the more likely it is that deviance will occur. The child from a family of low socioeconomic status (SES) is likely to value some behaviors which are not valued by his middle class teachers. The adolescent needs to please not only his parents and his teachers but his peers as well; it is likely that in pleasing one of these reference groups he may displease one of the others. Reference groups are particularly important in defining acceptable versus unacceptable behaviors because they are the repositories not only of the written and spoken rules which govern behavior, but these groups are also the source of the more numerous, and more important, unspoken and unwritten rules which govern behavior. Thus, school authorities may write rules which prohibit the wearing of jeans to schools and they may speak rules which prohibit the wearing of unusually tight clothing, but the more important expectation that students will come to school dressed is both unwritten and unspoken because it is considered so basic to the reference group expectations.

Deviance is often the result of particular behaviors, but thinking unusual thoughts and appearing unusual may also result in a person's being labeled deviant. Thus, handicapped persons are deviants who are given particular labels (blind, retarded, etc.) and restricted from certain privileges and opportunities (a form of punishment). Occasionally, a person's label may make deviant acts acceptable to the reference groups - thus, a narcotics agent may buy or sell illegal drugs if this is an aid to solving a crime.

2

Brilliant and talented individuals often think thoughts which no one else has thought - a form of deviance. However, once a person is labeled a "genius", unusual thought and action is expected of that individual and these unusual thoughts and actions are no longer seen as deviant by the reference group, which has given permission for unusualness, in a sense, in the form of a label. Thomas Edison (Dyer & Martin, 1929) was sent home by his primary school teacher with a note to his mother saying that because Tommy's brain was "addled" he was not to return to school. Albert Einstein experienced so many school failures that he did not complete his secondary school education and he failed the university admissions examination (Reiser, 1930).

Labels generate certain expectations from the reference group and these expectations are very resistant to change. Imagine a thirteen year old boy who has a school folder that is nearly five inches thick and who has been labeled as a disturbed, acting out student by numerous teachers. This boy, now in seventh grade, regularly begins his school days by running into his home room, slamming the door, aimlessly pulling open all of the teacher's desk drawers, upsetting the wastebasket, and hitting the smallest students in the class.

On one particular morning, however, this child calmly walks into his home room, stands near the teacher's desk, smiles at the teacher, and says "Good morning, how are you this morning?" What would be this teacher's reaction? Surely this would be classified as conforming behavior when emitted by most students. However, this boy's home room teacher is likely to be ready to duck at a moment's notice under these conditions. The teacher's thoughts are likely to be very hostile and suspicious, "You little brat, what are you up to now? Don't you start pulling a sweet act with me!" Thus, conforming behavior can be interpreted as deviant behavior when the reference group has labeled an individual deviant. Consequently, it is nearly impossible for a youngster caught in this situation to break out of a very vicious cycle.

Classroom Deviance as Necessary

Since it is impossible to anticipate every type of situation which may present itself, it is impossible for any reference group to have rules which will

3

proscribe all inappropriate behaviors. As every federal income tax payer knows, there are times when it
is necessary to take an educated, and optimistic,
guess as to what will be acceptable to the Internal
Revenue Service because the rules are either unclear
or nonexistent. Somewhat the same thing occurs in the
classroom. If a teacher is physically attacking a
child, is it right or wrong for that child to hit the
teacher? A child in this situation will act now and
ask questions later.

Erickson (1963) notes the following functions of
deviance: 1. deviance clarifies group norms; 2. deviance provides identity and cohesion for conformists;
3. deviance keeps the boundaries of group experience
flexible; 4. deviance provides impetus for changes in
norms; 5. deviance encourages creativity. Since one
of the pressures for conformity is the punishment of
deviance, children, as well as adults, must know what
happens to someone who breaks the rules if they are to
be fully motivated to follow those rules. Further,
individuals frequently group themselves according to
their perceptions of their own deviance or conformity.
Thus, "good" students tend to associate with "good"
students and poor students tend to associate with one
another. Dissatisfied teachers tend to associate with
other dissatisfied teachers; these teachers talk together in the teachers room, they go to bars together, they visit one another's homes and talk about the
confused thinking of the satisfied teachers. Mean-
while, of course, the satisfied teachers are party ing
together and talking about the befuddlement of the
dissatisfied teachers. These differences in teacher
orientation lead to a team spirit for those of similar
ilk. The formation of subgroups of teachers within a
school or district also makes life more zestful for
everyone by providing an endless source of gossip,
jokes, and general speculation. Much the same type of
thing happens as a result of student groupings!

Deviance also keeps the boundaries of group experience flexible. This phenomenon is particularly
well illustrated by the omnipresence of pot smoking.
Although the selling of marijuana is still illegal,
many states have made possession of small amounts of
marijuana a misdemeanor rather than a felony in response to the fact it is impractical and undesirable
to accuse and prosecute a near majority of U.S. citizens for a felony. There are many who believe that
the laws which prohibit the use of marijuana will

4

someday be repealed in the same way that laws which
prohibited the use of alcohol eventually had to be repealed - largely because of widespread disobedience.

Creativity is deviant by definition since that
which is truly creative departs significantly from the
accepted ways of thinking and acting. It seems likely
that societies with high rates of deviant behavior may
also be societies which are stronger in creative
fields of endeavor. The United States, which has a
relatively high crime rate, is very highly respected
in almost every country in the world, including the
Soviet Union, for its creative technology and for its
music. Rollo May, a well-known psychoanalyst, has
written a book entitled The Courage to Create in which
he makes the following observation;

> Consciousness is the awareness that
> emerges out of the dialetical tensions be-
> tween possibilities and limitations. In-
> fants begin to be aware of limits when they
> experience the ball as different from them-
> selves; mother is a limiting factor for them
> in that she does not feed them every time
> they cry for food. Through a multitude of
> such limiting experiences they learn to de-
> velop the capacity to differentiate them-
> selves from others and from objects and to
> delay gratification. If there had been no
> limits, there would be no consciousness.
>
> Our discussion so far may seem, at
> first glance, to be discouraging, but not
> when we probe more deeply. It is not by
> accident that the Hebrew myth that marks the
> beginning of human consciousness, Adam and
> Eve in the Garden of Eden, is portrayed in
> the context of a rebellion. Consciousness
> is born in the struggle against a limit,
> called there a prohibition. Going beyond
> the limit set by Yahweh is then punished by
> the acquiring of other limits which operate
> inwardly in the human being - anxiety, the
> feeling of alienation and guilt. But valu-
> able qualities also come out of this expe-
> rience of rebellion - the sense of personal
> responsibility and ultimately the possibili-
> ty, born out of loneliness, of human love.

(Rollo May, Pg. 114-115, 1975)

Although one of the major goals of this book is an examination of techniques of control for deviant classroom behaviors, yet another goal is a serious examination of the desirability of deviant behavior. The teacher must not only ask, "How do I extinguish this behavior," but also, "Is it desirable to extinguish this behavior - however deviant it may seem."

Desirable Deviance

In later chapters we shall examine control measures for typically undesirable school misbehaviors. However, the fact that all school misbehaviors are not undesirable can not be overstated. The farmer who blindly kills all insects will have a pest free garden, but the crop may be lost for lack of pollination since beneficial insects will also have been exterminated. The elimination of undesirable behavior is an important part of the educational process, but misbehaviors must be selectively eliminated or the social and intellectual growth of students and teachers may be stunted.

Deviant behavior can amuse, stimulate, inform and promote personal growth, independence, and empathy. Four primary types of school deviance may be identified. These four types are (1) intentional physical or mental harm to others; (2) interferring with school work; (3) thinking, acting, or appearing unusual; (4) damaging property. Naturally, these three types may be broadly or narrowly defined. For example, is a punch on the arm "physical harm?"

Even the most repulsive form of school misbehavior, the infliction of deliberate physical or mental harm, can sometimes be excused as desirable deviance. If a four foot tall, eighty pound weakling made a daily habit of "beating on" a taller, heavier, and stronger schoolmate during recess, the silent sufferer would not get much sympathy from school authorities, who would expect him to teach the younger and smaller boy a lesson himself rather than constantly running to the teachers and principals for help. Spankings which are administered by principals in the presence of a witness are examples of intentional physical, or mental, harm which are generally socially approved and which are legally acceptable (Ingraham vs. Wright, 1977, Supreme Court decision).

Less serious forms of school deviance can be fun

6

and exciting for teachers and students alike. In fact, deviant behavior which is sufficiently clever and entertaining will usually be viewed as acceptable behavior. Such a metamorphosis of behavior occurred in a school for emotionally disturbed adolescents when several of these youngsters rightly noted that their young bachelor principal had a chronic case of bad breath. Rather than coming nose to nose with the principal and saying, "You know, your breath stinks!", these enterprising deviants entered the teachers' lounge at lunch time and good humoredly got the teachers to sign their names to a Christmas card for the principal. The students themselves never signed the card and the principal's Christmas present, presented with the teachers' signatures, was a very large bottle of mouth wash - which amused everyone except the principal.

A well known principle of educational psychology is that a moderately high level of physiological arousal facilitates memory. If a colleague says, "hello", when he passes you in the hallway, it is unlikely that you will recall this greeting next week because it is a very ordinary event which does not invite physiological arousal. However, if you are very angry at this person or if he waves both arms and rolls his eyes when saying hello, you may well remember the event next week because your level of physiological arousal was heightened at the time of the greeting. School deviance often results in the learning of unforgettable lessons, as in the case of a learning disabled ten year old who was engaging in the school sport of the month, which involved throwing wet paper towels at the ceiling and getting them to stick there. This unlucky youth broke a light to smithereens by hitting it with a cold, wet paper towel. When he got over his shattering conviction that God had miraculously punished him, he learned a lesson he never forgot, e.g., that hot glass breaks when touched by something cold. Further, all of the other children in the school learned the same lesson, which they have hopefully remembered.

Verbal arguments in the classroom are often seen as unruly deviant behavior that interferes with school work, work which many teachers prefer to see as "correct" or "incorrect". Since teachers are often led to believe that their job is the preparation of students for achievement tests and competency tests, all of which operate on the assumption of "correctness" and

7

"incorrectness", their emphasis on a black and white model is to some extent justified. Research indicates that classroom conflict is strongly discouraged (DeCecco & Richards, 1974), even though a lively controversy can facilitate learning, increase creativity, and promote problem solving abilities (Johnson & Johnson, 1979). Johnson and Johnson present an example of controversy from a social studies class:

> ... a teacher is presenting a lesson on the United States Congress. The students are discussing in small groups the reasons why citizens want to be representatives in Congress. One student says the major reason is wanting to help your neighbors and your country. Another student says being a member of Congress is just a way to get rich, and quotes Roger Mudd (CBS News, December 24, 1976) that a representative in Congress receives more than $400,000 per year in salary and benefits. Voices rise as the argument continues. What does the teacher do? Would the teacher encourage the argument, helping students find evidence to support and argue their positions? Or would the teacher try to calm things down and change the topic or discussion?

(Johnson & Johnson, 1979, p. 51)

Johnson and Johnson observe that, unfortunately, most teachers would try to calm things down in whatever way possible.

Children who are gifted or retarded are often excluded from regular classrooms on the basis of their unusual learning behaviors and children with severe burn scars or skeletal deformities are often excluded because of their unusual and stigmatizing appearance. Recently federal law (P.L. 94-142) has mandated that all children be placed in the least restrictive environment possible and the result has been a heavy emphasis on the mainstreaming of exceptional, i.e., deviant children. Although there have been many justifications cited for the trend to mainstreaming, only a few of these considerations will concern us here. One effect of mainstreaming is very similar to that of racial integration; namely, this approach provides an opportunity for cross pollination between traditionally segregated groups, an opportunity to learn about

8

one another and, hopefully, an opportunity to accept
and appreciate one another. When exceptional, or deviant, individuals are placed in segregated situations, the social expectations and the social behaviors of the segregated group become significantly different from the social expectations and behaviors of
typical persons because the group differences are
mirrored and magnified through association with similar others. Thus, the retarded can be expected to become more retarded because intellectual stimulation is
decreased, and the gifted can be expected to become
more brilliant because intellectual stimulation is increased. The physically handicapped can be expected
to find it more difficult to associate with the typical children from whom they have been segregated and
the typical children can be expected to find it more
difficult to feel comfortable with handicapped persons
with whom they have had no previous contact. On the
other hand, integrating children who are different
with children who are typical may foster the growth of
empathy, confidence, and understanding for all students.

"Reverse mainstreaming" is a term which has been
used to describe the situation in which a typical
child is placed in a classroom for exceptional children for part of the day. This not only helps to des-
tigmatize a classroom by making it obvious that all
kinds of kids go to that room, not just the "dumb"
ones, but it also creates a different reference group
situation, and, in a sense, forces the typical child
to seek acceptance from those she might ordinarily
think of as inferiors. In this situation, the typical
child is a minority group member who must acquiesce to
the expectations of the, in this case, deviant social
group. This temporary reversal in roles provides a
learning situation for both typical and exceptional
children.

Bowen (1978) has indicated that deviant behavior
may be important in developing a differentiation of
the self from what he calls the "undifferentiated
family ego mass", in which family members do not acknowledge one another's individuality. There are many
common personality problems which lead individuals to
act as if their wishes, feelings and desires were the
standard against which reality should be judged. This
often leads to a confusion of subjective perceptions
and actual events.

9

Indeed, healthy young children naturally pass through a similar stage which they should later outgrow. For example, very young children tend to see their primary caretakers, usually their mothers, as all powerful. Therefore, if a social agency should remove a young child from the home, the child will often perceive that the parent has sent her away, a perfectly logical conclusion if the parent were actually all powerful. The child often concludes that the only reason a parent would send a child away would be if the child were "bad". The sent away child then introjects a self-definition of "badness". The important consequences of such a self definition will be examined in later chapters. However, the importance of subjective feeling in the interpretation of reality can not be over stressed. Adults who can not separate their own ego's from those of others may see unruly students acting hatefully and spitefully towards them while, in reality, the students' behaviors have nothing whatever to do with those adults. Such adults may also increase the level of youngsters' deviant behaviors by making it necessary for such youngsters to protest their own individuality by rebelling against the wishes and desires of immature or egocentric adults.

Any understanding of deviant behavior requires an understanding of the forces which lead most of us to conform to reference group expectations most of the time. We shall now turn our attention to conforming behavior.

References

Bowen, M. Family Therapy in Clinical Practice. New York: Jason Aronson, 1978.

De Cecco, J., & Richards, A. Growing Pains: Uses of School Conflict. New York: Aberdeen Press, 1974

Dyer, F.L., & Martin, T.C. Edison: His Life and Inventions, Vols. I and II. New York: Harper & Brothers, 1929.

Erikson, K.T. Wayward Puritans. New York: John Wiley & Sons, 1963.

Johnson, D.W., & Johnson, R.T. Conflict in the Classroom: Controversy and Learning. Review of Educational Research, 1979, 49, 1, 51-70.

May, R. The Courage to Create. New York: W.W. Norton, 1975.

Chapter Two

AN INTRODUCTION TO CONFORMITY

Although each of us spends considerable amounts of time engaging in conforming behaviors and in trying to get members of our social groups to conform to group expectations, conformity is generally viewed as a ho hum phenomenon by lay persons and by sociologists alike. Innumerable books have been written about deviant behavior, but hardly any books at all have examined conforming behavior. Definitions of conformity appear to suffer from the difficulties that have always plagued theological definitions of the "good." Theologians, for lack of a better definition, have frequently found it necessary to define the "good" as the "absence of evil." Similarly, conformity is sometimes little more than the absence of deviance.

Perhaps the best known and most widely accepted definition of conformity is that which was put forward by Robert Merton, a well-known sociologist. Merton (1957) notes that individuals most commonly adapt to social expectations by conforming to those expectations, which means that these individuals accept cultural goals while also accepting the institutionalized means of working towards those goals. Merton believes that the primary cultural goal in the U.S. society is success and the institutionalized means are getting an education and working hard. Since the primary function of the school is the transmission of the dominant culture, including the goals of that culture, as well as the history, language, values and beliefs of that culture, the schools are indispensible in the development of conformity, as defined by Merton. Multicultural education acknowledges the existence and validity of other cultures, but the primary goal of the school, even in a situation where a multi-cultural education is provided, is to help the student adapt to the dominant culture.

Obviously, if a student conforms to the cultural goals and instutionalized means of our society, s/he probably will not be a school discipline problem. Such a student will value an education and will work diligently at school related tasks. In addition to conforming to the goals of the dominant culture, the student is also expected to conform to the goals of specific schools, classrooms and peer groups. Persons

13

who are not familiar with the inner workings of the schools often think of conformity primarily in terms of students complying with teachers' demands in the classroom. Though conformity within the classroom situation is of great interest, it is important to remember that it is often more important to the physical and mental well-being of students that they conform to peer group demands than to teacher demands. For example, in one inner city school, the subcultural goal was the domination of white students by black students; the means for the achievement of that goal were set by blacks, who expected whites to conform. Each day the criterion for avoiding a beating was changed. One day, for example, black students would declare that all whites must carry four leaf clovers (of undesignated composition, of course) on their person and white students would be stopped by black students for an inspection of the four leaf clovers. On very difficult days, blacks might initially establish a requirement for possession of a rabbit's foot and, later in the day change it to a requirement for a red ribbon. Although school personnel did not favor this system of intimidation, it was obviously to the benefit of both students and faculty for the minority white students to comply with the demands of the well organized black students. When considering the school situation, it is as important to examine conformity to the goals and means of subcultures and of smaller social groups as it is to examine conformity to the goals and means of the dominant culture.

Influences to Conformity

Hirschi (1969) lists four influences to conformity: 1. attachment to others; 2. previous personal investment in socially acceptable goal directed activity; 3. overwhelming preoccupation with socially acceptable activity; 4. acceptance of the morality of social rules. One might add passivity and Maslow's (1948) hierachy of physical needs, safety needs, and self-esteem needs to Hirschi's list of influences to conformity. The implications for the schools of these influences to conformity will now be examined.

Basic Human Needs

Although human beings can subordinate their basic human needs to intellectual ideals, as in the case of a hunger strike, when the need for food may be subordinated to a desire to achieve a social goal, this is

14

not a common occurence. Physical needs for food, shelter, etc., generally outweigh other considerations in the determination of acts of conformity or of deviance. The science of behavior modification, the practice of which often utilizes primary reinforcers, such as food, is adequate testimony to the fact that a manipulation of the satisfaction of basic needs can elicit conforming behaviors.

Yet another example of the strength of basic human needs is that although educated Anglo (English speaking, white) individuals in the United States tend to see multi-cultural education as an intellectually honest and morally desirable improvement over the past unyielding insistence on a melting pot society, many of the groups for whom multi-cultural programs have been developed express grave concern about such programs. For example, many blacks believe that the continued use of Black English, rather than Standard English, by black youngsters will lead to difficulties in obtaining employment and, thereby, in fulfilling the basic needs for food, shelter and safety. Many blacks would prefer to conform to the language expectations of the dominant culture rather than risk employment difficulties; many spanish speaking parents seem to have similar concerns about bilingual programs.[1]

Social Needs

The human needs for affiliation and affection require some degree of conformity to the expectations of others, who expect their needs to be met in particular groups of people. For example, students expect school to be a serious place where learning occurs; if the school does not fulfill these expectations, student behavior will be chaotic and/or destructive. Goffman (1959) notes that, "... the structure of social encounters ... is the maintenance of a simple definition of the situation ... sustained in the face of a multitude of potential disruptions," (p. 254). Thus it is that we attempt to monitor others' perceptions of ourselves and others' perceptions of our perceptions as well as our perceptions of their perceptions of our perceptions, ad infinitum.

Teachers know that students tend to test the

---

[1] Comments made to the author by Black and Spanish speaking parents in the Chicago area.

social limits of the classroom during the first few weeks of the school year. Consequently, most teachers try to be unusually strict and serious during those first few weeks in order to get their students to perceive them as teachers who mean business and who impose well-defined rules and expectations. Teachers also try to control students' perceptions of their perceptions of the students; for example, an impromptu joke from a student during serious class discussion might result in appreciative laughter from the teacher during the middle of the school year, but the same teacher might well remain quite poker faced at a joke made during the first few weeks of school, the message being that students have come to school to learn and not to joke around.

Some form of impression management is probably always necessary, but the maintenance of a front is particularly important when the social participants know little of one another:

> The more information the audience has about the performer, the less likely it is that anything they learn during the interaction will radically influence them. On the other hand, where no prior information is possessed, it may may be expected that the information gleaned during the interaction will be relatively crucial. Hence, on the whole, we may expect individuals to relax the strict maintenance of front when they are with those they have known for a long time, and to tighten their front when among persons who are new to them. With those whom one does not know, careful performances are required.

> (Goffman, 1959, p.222)

Of course, students as well as teachers engage in impression management by performing as they wish to be perceived. In some cases, students who have difficulty in trusting others may deliberately put their worst foot forward in an attempt at determining whether they can expect rejection from the teacher. If the teacher is able to firmly maintain high standards of behavior while also conveying a sense of interpersonal acceptance, such students will often develop enough trust in the teacher that they will be able to conform to the teacher's expectations. More will be said of

16

methods of developing interpersonal trust in later chapters.

Except for the value of a given behavior to the actor, attachment to others may well be the most influential factor in bringing about conformity. Tittle (1977) sampled 2,000 households and found that:

> ... fear of losing respect among people one knows personally ranks second only to the utility of the behavior ... the data suggest that perceptions of the probability of community exposure or of arrest and incarceration have no greater effect on the likelihood of deviance than does the probability of simple discovery by somebody who would not approve the behavior.
>
> (Tittle, 1977, p. 592)

Consequently, conforming behaviors are likely to occur when an individual has developed an emotional attachment to persons whose values support such behaviors. It should not be surprising that the approval and disapproval of others should dictate conformity since every individual is dependent on others for a confirmation of self, "All 'identities' require an other: some other in and through a relationship with whom self-identity is actualized," (Laing, 1971, p. 82).

The importance of others in determining self-worth is almost overwhelming for young children and for those who are not emotionally mature, or who do not have adequate ego differentiation. Young children do not have adequate ego differentiation. Young children do not have the verbal cushions which adults possess. If an adult is told that she is stupid, she will usually be able to remember many instances in which others told her she was brilliant. With the use of pleasant recollections, this woman will be able to develop a verbal cushion for the put down she is currently experiencing. "Well, you, in your ignorance, think that I am stupid, but I know better because I have had many experiences which have proven my intelligence". Children, however, do not have this experiential background on which to fall and they are considerably more at the mercy of the judgements of others than are adults. For example, the author once observed four or five ten year old boys and a seven year old boy sitting at a round table in a deli. The

17

children were discussing the fact that school was to start in two or three weeks.
"Oh, yuck, school starts soon."
"Yeah, I hate school!"
"School stinks!"
At this point the seven year old piped up, "I like school!"
"He likes school! Oh, boy, he's stupid!"
"Yeah, you're stupid!"
"You're dumb if you like school!"
"But I'm only going into second grade!"
It seems likley that by third grade, this seven year old boy will indeed hate school, and such is the stuff of conformity. The schools respond to this obvious problem by mobilizing a cadre of door-to-door salespeople. Teachers furtively knock for admittance to students' minds with pathetic comments like, "Don't you like school? Isn't school fun! Getting an education is so important!" If General Motors abandoned all sleek advertising and attempted to sell cars with door to door salespeople, our economy would, indeed, be in big trouble, but schools regularly sell their wares in just this way. Children who can be convinced that they absolutely must have Jupiter Rocks for breakfast could surely be convinced that they like school, and this positive attitude would surely result in improved performance in school - both behaviorally and cognitively.

Envelopment in the Socially Acceptable

Most people are so heavily involved in socially acceptable goal directed activity that they have too little time to even consider deviant behavior; they have been so engaged for so long that they have developed an investment in conforming behaviors. The "straight A" student often is considerably more concerned about getting an "A" in a course than is the student who actually needs an "A" for a passing grade point average. Experienced teachers generally acknowledge the importance of providing students with success experiences in avoiding discipline problems; in addition, such teachers also realize that a student who is constantly busy completing assignments will not have the time to act-up.

However, persons who have not been successful in achieving socially acceptable goals are not able to develop an investment in conforming behaviors. As a result there is a considerable amount of evidence which indicates that for some youth the emphasis on staying in school is not only mistaken but also counter-productive. School attendance may actually result in higher delinquency rates than dropping out of school (Elliot, 1968; Elliot & Voss, 1973; Empey, Lubeck, & LaPorte, 1971). Youth who are failing in school, but who remain in school, are faced with the problem of salvaging their self-esteem and of having enough fun to compensate for the daily humiliations to which they are subject. Such youth are more than likely to meet peers with the same needs and problems within the school situation since the schools regularly group students according to their achievement levels. The emphasis which adults, and particularly educators, place on getting along with others alerts youth to the importance of peer group conformity - this probably enhances the likelihood of participation in delinquent activities. Strangely, not much attention has been given to schools as intact social systems; it is not known, for example, whether there are some schools which foster deviant activities and others which tend to foster conforming behaviors.

School climate does seem to have a significant effect on achievement (Brookover, et al., 1978) and, presumably, it may have a similar effect on the prevalence of socially acceptable, conforming, behaviors. School climate has been defined as follows:

> The school social climate encompasses a composite of variables as defined and perceived by members of this group. These factors may be broadly conceived as the norms of the social system and expectations held for various members as perceived by the members of the group and communicated to members of the group.

> (Brookover & Erickson, 1975, p. 364)

Brookover, et al., (1978) note that a given school's climate, or subculture, seems to be highly related to the climate of particular classrooms, accounting for 43 percent of the variance between classrooms. Brookover, et al., observe that low SES (socio-economic status) and the racial composition of a school may not be as important for academic achievement as is school climate:

Predominantly low SES and minority schools

19

are more likely to be characterized by a high sense of student academic futility, low academic norms and low expectations for and evaluations of the students. In fact, these composition characteristics frequently may contribute to the development of differential expectations, norms, and feelings of futility. But these composition variables do not invariably produce such climate differences. Favorable climate rather than specific composition is, we believe, the necessary condition for high achievement.

(Brookover, et al., 1978, pp. 316-317)

Thus, both students and teachers seem to conform to the school climate, or subculture. This conformity to a school climate appears to have rather dramatic effects on school achievement. Findings of the study of Brookover, et al., indicate that schools with counterproductive school climates may "write off" larger numbers of students than do schools with favorable school climates these researchers found that schools with counterproductive climates tended to group large numbers of students in a slow group, for which teachers had very low achievement expectations. Schools with subcultures, or climates, which were favorable to achievement tended to encourage team competion in academics, rather than individual competition. Students in schools with favorable climates received immediate positive reinforcement for correct answers, but students in schools with counter- productive climates often received no reinforcement for incorrect answers. Unfortunately, the origins of school climate are not yet understood, but this construct obviously has serious implications for conforming behaviors within the school and classroom.

It seems likely that the values and norms which students encounter on first entering a school, or classroom, tend to be self-perpetuating. Students who perceive that this school is a joke where only the tough guys survive will neglect achievement and fall further behind in academics, with the result that they will be turned-off to academics because they are so far behind. On the other hand, students who get the idea that students in this school are really serious about school work will perceive that their own social acceptance may require that they also be serious about school work, and, in being serious, they dis-

20

cover that learning has its rewards. Similarly, teachers quickly establish self-perpetuating habits of instruction, such as home preparation versus nonpreparation, time spent interacting directly with students versus time spent hiding behind the desk, etc.

Teachers also establish peer pressure groups. For example, the author was once visited in her classroom by a fairly large group of disgruntled teachers who informed her in no uncertain terms that they needed their morning and afternoon breaks. At the time, a teacher's aide was being sent into each classroom for about twenty minutes in the morning and in the afternoon - at which time teachers could presumably take a break. The author preferred to work individually with students at these times, but other teachers feared that some administrator might interpret this as an indication that teachers didn't really need breaks. Obviously, teachers, as well as students, are expected to conform to socially acceptable behaviors, as these are defined in a given school.

Morality of Social Rules

A belief in the morality of social rules can motivate conforming behavior. An individual's convictions of "rightness" and "wrongness" are largely determined by an individual's intellectual development (Kohlberg & Turiel, 1971; Piaget & Inhelder, 1969); however, an individual's actions need not be in conformity with her convictions. Presumably, though, most people act in accordance with their convictions of morality most of the time. Kohlberg and Turiel (1971) have identified six sequential stages of moral development: stage one involves unquestioning obedience to authority in order to avoid punishment, a stage which is characteristic of young children; stage two involves a perception of "rightness" as an even exchange, "if you do something for me, I'll do something for you"; stage three persons attempt to obtain the approval of others; stage four stresses a fixed notion of law and order; stage five persons see morality in terms of a social contract which may be changed through mutual agreement; stage six persons conform to self-chosen ethical principles that are universally applicable. Kohlberg and Turiel (1971) believe that most adults are at stages four and five - with very few adults being at stage six. Obviously, a person at stage six could be quite troublesome in any social system, whether of a nation, community, or school, be-

21

cause she tends to act independently of the rules of the social system, while still acting in the best interest of all individuals: Christ, Martin Luther King, Jr., and Gandhi are examples of such persons.

It may be that most schools address the student body, and perhaps the faculty, as if all individuals involved were at stage three. Teachers and administrators often attempt to control others though simple approval and disapproval. This approach may work with individuals who are at this stage of moral development, but it probably will not work with those who are not at that stage. Adolescents are frequently found at stage three, but the significant others that adolescents primarily attempt to please are their peers, who often hold values which are in conflict with those held by school authorities.

Schools might be more effective in eliciting conforming behaviors from students if they attempted to differentiate "right" from "wrong" in accordance with a student's level of moral development. Schools attempt to teach academic subject matter at each student's achievement level, but there is usually no attempt made at gearing moral directives to a student's developmental level in the area of moral reasoning.

Self-esteem

Self-esteem is generally defined as self-acceptance (Bergin & Lambert, 1978). As was noted in the discussion of the effects of social needs on conforming behaviors, the opinions of others are instrumental in determining the way one perceives oneself. There is some empirical evidence that deviant, or nonconforming, behaviors are preceded by self-rejection (Kaplan, 1975; 1977):

> Negative self-attitudes are the consequence of a history of adverse experiences in the person's membership group(s) that culminate in self-perceptions of failing to possess positively valued behaviors, self-perceptions as the object of negative attitudes expressed by valued others, and the inability to effectively employ self-protective mechanisms in the face of self-devaluating experiences. The person comes to perceive the association and, ultimately,

22

to intrinsically disvalue the response patterns endorsed by the membership group(s). Since the individual is characterized by the experience of subjectively distressful negative self-attitudes he is motivated to seek alternative response patterns to the now disvalued normatively endorsed patterns that would function to reduce the experience of self-rejecting attitudes. Deviant responses represent such alternative attempts to reduce the consequent high levels of self-- rejecting attitudes through fostering avoidance of prior self-devaluing experiences, attack upon the basis of one's self-- rejecting attitudes, and the opportunity for self-enhancement through substitute experiences.

(Kaplan, 1977, pp. 77, 78)

Accordingly, schools which expose students and/or teachers to experiences of personal rejection may expect high levels of nonconforming, or deviant, behavior. Conversely, schools which provide a general atmosphere of acceptance should develop high levels of conforming behaviors.

The specific implications of the preceding include the fact that schools which identify large numbers of students as academic failures may expect high levels of deviant behavior. If socially acceptable behaviors are to be fostered in the school situation, it is imperative that schools make group membership a pleasant experience.

Passivity

Conforming behaviors probably most often occur as a result of passivity. Conforming behavior generally requires less expenditure of energy than does deviant behavior, particularly since deviant behavior is often followed by long lasting unpleasant consequences. Often, those who conform to social rules lose sight of the reasons for conforming:

We seem to need to share a communal meaning to human existence, to give with others a common sense to the world, to maintain a consensus.

But it seems that once certain fundamental structures of experience are shared,
they come to be experienced as objective en-
tities... They take on the force and character of partially autonomous realities, with
their own way of life. A social norm may
come to impose an oppressive obligation on
everyone, although few people feel it as
their own.

. . .

Everyone will be carrying out orders. Where
do they come from? Always from elsewhere.

(Laing, 1967, pp. 77,78)

Obvious problems in accountability can arise when
orders always come from "elsewhere." In retrospect,
for example, orders for pograms always seem to have
come from elsewhere. Persons who are particularly
prone to following orders which come from elsewhere
include those in the first four or five Kohlberg
stages of moral development; persons in stage six
accept responsibility for their own behavior since the
ethical principles they employ are self-chosen, but it
must be remembered that only a small number of adults
are able to operate at this level.

Since many of the most important decisions in education are made by state and local boards of education, a great many orders in the schools do come from
"elsewhere." Further, since boards of education are
often comprised of laypersons, the professional educators who must implement prescribed social norms, or
rules, often feel these to be an oppressive obligation
and not in keeping with their own convictions. Such a
state of affairs may lead to students perceiving
teachers and principals as hypocrites since they enforce rules they often disdain, as in the case of
school board imposed rules relative to dress code and
hair length, for example. It might be noted that
boards of education are a vestige of the church related Board of Selectmen which used to be responsible
for various community concerns, including the hiring
of teachers, in the colonial days of the United States
(Goldhammer, 1964). Since little, or nothing was
known regarding the science of education, or of related disciplines, in those days, leaving the schools
in the hands of laypersons did not create a conflict
of interest. However, it might be argued that placing

24

the schools in the hands of laypersons in the late 20th century is analogous to encouraging consumers to direct the activities of large corporations because they have been consumers for all of their lives and it is therefore concluded that they are now experts in business management. Laypersons often believe that the experience of having been a student has made them experts in education, and this conviction is strengthened by the relative lack of abstruse jargon among professional educators, which results in the layperson's being able to understand all of the words being used by educators, with the often erroneous assumption being that all of the concepts have been understood as well.

Passivity in the schools, relative to conforming behaviors, can result from the fact that people feel obligated to carry out orders which come from elsewhere, but passivity can also be a direct result of the reward structure of the school and classroom. There are some indications that teachers often grade students on their academic competence based not on their actual academic performance, but, rather, based on their classroom behavior (Brophy & Good, 1974; Gravenberg & Collins, 1976). Thus, the passive student who rides the tide and conforms to classroom expectations in his social behaviors may receive very acceptable school grades even if he is also very passive in his academic work and learns very little. Often, a teacher's primary concern is simply that a student not disrupt the class so that those who do wish to learn may do so, and so students are rewarded for not disrupting the class rather than for learning academics.

Functions of Conformity in the School

Obviously, neither the school nor any other social institution could function if most of its members did not conform most of the time. Indeed, school personnel often overlook the fact that even those youngsters with the worst behavior problems do conform most of the time. Interestingly, and fortunately, persons who are less intelligent and less competent will generally conform to the opinions of those who are more intelligent and more competent (Crutchfield, 1955; Lucito, 1964, Madison & Conner, 1973). Consequently, the human tendency to conform may result in a somewhat higher level of overall social functioning both in the classroom and in the larger society.

Conformity allows a sense of "we-ness" to develop between group members. This we-ness is so important that sports teams and many fraternal groups, for example, are expected to wear nearly identical uniforms in an attempt at developing a sense of we-ness which is obvious not only to the members themselves but to the audience as well. Conformity is required if individuals are to cohere in a social group. The we-ness which develops from such conformity provides each member of the group with the assurance of support from others in the group. Studies of the effects of interpersonal co-operation, versus competition or individualistic efforts, in learning tasks have indicated that students who engage in problem solving under co-operative conditions often outperform students who engage in similar problem solving under competitive or individualistic conditions, perhaps, in part, because students in co-operative groups perceive greater support and encouragement for achievement under co-operative conditions (Johnson, Skon, & Johnson, 1980). Further, co-operative conditions eliminate the probability that a majority of the students will be "losers," as is almost necessarily the case under competitive conditions, and usually the case under individualistic conditions. Students who repeatedly "lose" in academic activities can be expected to stop playing this humiliating game and to devote themselves to activities which are more self-enhancing, often these are activities which deviate from the norms established by the school. Consequently, co-operative activities can be expected to make group membership more attractive to a majority of students and this can be expected to lead to ever greater conformity because group membership is highly valued since this helps everyone to become a winner. Individualistic and competitive activities, on the other hand, will probably lead to ever decreasing levels of conformity as losing participants lose interest in participating and as winning participants develop a vested interest in maintaining their lead, obviously at the expense of others. It is interesting to note that most school activities involve individualistic and competitive conditions rather than co-operative conditions. If the increasing complexities of our technological society lead to an increasing emphasis on co-operation, as exemplified by the ubiquitous committee, it would seem appropriate for the schools to begin emphasizing co-operative endeavors in classroom learning, rather than the traditional individualistic and competitive approaches to learning. As previously

26

discussed, an emphasis on co-operative approaches group learning could be expected to reduce the number of classroom behavior problems.

Once a social group establishes a sense of we-ness, however, it often becomes necessary for the group to differentiate itself from other groups, to establish its own self-identity, as it were. As an example of this, Erikson (1963) notes that, "It was exactly because the New England Puritans shared so many features in common with the Quakers that they had to publicise the few crucial differences as noisily as they could," (p. 126). Consequently, co-operative group learning may soon turn into competitive group learning as groups establish individual identities. In order to avoid this phenomenon, friendship patterns within the school and the classroom must be diffuse, overlapping between groups, rather than centrally structured (Schmuck & Schmuck, 1975; Sites, 1973). If students' identities become dependent upon their membership in a given group, competition between groups is inevitable; however, if individuals have diffuse membership patterns and belong to several groups, groups will avoid conflict and attempt to cooperate with one another (Sites, 1973). Thus, educators should use flexible grouping patterns and they should avoid establishing well-delineated and permanent groupings of students.

Dysfunctions of Conformity in the School

The attempts of the school at teaching independent thinking and individual responsibility are at odds with perfect conformity. As was discussed earlier in the present chapter, Kohlberg's highest stage of moral development is one in which the individual conforms to his own self-chosen ethical principles rather than to the expectations of others, and such behavior often more closely resembles deviance than it resembles conformity. In addition, there are some indications that creative thinking may be negatively correlated with conforming behaviors (Illingworth, 1975; Stone, 1980; Wallach & Kogan, 1965). Since conforming behaviors generally maintain the status quo, it might also be argued that deviant behaviors are necessary if change and progress are to occur.

A review of the literature (Johnson & Johnson, 1979) indicates that conflict in the classroom can produce, under the appropriate conditions, a number of

27

desirable outcomes:

> Disagreement among students' ideas, conclusions, theories, and opinions is an important source of learning in all instructional situations. ... there is evidence that such conflicts will create conceptual conflict, feelings of uncertainty and epistemic curiosity; increase students accuracy of cognitive perspective-taking; promote students transitions from one stage of cognitive and moral reasoning to another; increase the quality of students' problem solving; and, increase students' creativeness.

(p. 62)

Despite the obvious advantages of the appropriate use of conflict in the classroom, there are indications that teachers tend to avoid the free expression of conflicting opinions in the classroom (De Cecco & Richards, 1974; Johnson & Johnson, 1979). A cooperative, rather than a competitive, context is required for constructive controversy to occur (Johnson, 1974; Johnson & Johnson, 1975). However, teachers may often interpret conflict as undesirable aggressive behavior and attempt to steer student thinking in the direction of conformity. Unfortunately, educators may tend to equate co-operativeness with conformity. In a think tank situation, the expression of conflict under co-operative conditions is essential, and such an approach could enhance the educational process in the schools.

When no conflict exists, there may be a tendency for it to be created. For example, there is some evidence that presenting anti-drug abuse information to students whose own views are in conformity with the message of such programs may result in a boomerang effect in which students develop positive attitudes towards drug use (Feingold & Knapp, 1977; Halpin & Whiddon, 1977). It may be that educators need to be aware of a satiation level for conforming behaviors and attitudes so that care may be taken lest such satiation occur inappropriately.

References

Bergin, A., & Lambert, M. The evaluation of therapeutic outcomes. In S. Garfield and A. Bergin (Eds) Handbook of psychotherapy and Behavior change: An empirical analysis. New York: John Wiley & Sons, 1978.

Brookover, W., & Erickson, E. Sociology of education. Homewood, Illinois; Dorsey Press, 1975.

Brookover, W., Schweitzer, J., Schneider, J., Beady, C., Flood, P., Wisenbaker, J. Elementary school social climate and school achievement. American Educational Research Journal, 1978, 15, 301-318.

Brophy, J., & Good, T. Teacher-student relationships; Causes and consequences. New York: Holt, Rinehart & Winston, 1974.

Crutchfield, R.S. Conformity and character. American Psychologist, 1955, 10, 191-198.

DeCecco, J., & Richards, A. Growing pains: Uses of school conflict. New York: Aberdeen Press, 1974.

Elliot, D. Delinquency, school attendance and dropout. In. J. Stratton (Ed.) Prevention of delinquency: Problems and programs. New York: MacMillan, 1968, 191-199.

Elliot, D., & Voss, H. Delinquency and dropout. Lexington, Mass.: D.C. Heath, 1974.

Empey, L., LaPorte, R., & Lubeck, S. Explaining delinquency. Lexington, Mass.: D.C. Heath & Co., 1971.

Erikson, K.T. Wayward puritans. New York: Wiley & Sons, 1963.

Feingold, P., & Knapp, M. Anti-drug abuse commercials. Journal of Communication, 1977, 27, 20-28.

Goffman, E. The presentation of self in everyday life. New York: Doubleday, 1959.

Goldhammer, K. The school board. New York: Center for Applied Research in education, 1964.

References

Gravenberg, O., & Collins, G. Grades: Just a measure of conformity. Humboldt Journal of Social Relations, 1976, 3, 58-62.

Halpin, G., & Whiddon, T. Drug education: Solution or problem? Psychological Reports, 1977, 40, 372-374.

Hirschi, T. Causes of delinquency. Berkeley: University of California Press, 1969.

Illingworth, R.R. Lessons from childhood. (Excerpt from article presented at the First Wordl Council for Gifted CHildren in London, 1975, as quoted in N/S-LTI-G/T Bulletin, 1977, 4, 3.)

Johnson, D. Communication and the inducement of cooperative behavior in conflicts. Speech Monographs, 1974, 41, 64-78.

Johnson, D., & Johnson, R. Learning together and alone: Cooperation, competition, and individualization. Englewood Cliffs, N.J.: Prentice-Hall, 1975.

Johnson, D., & Johnson, R. Conflict in the classroom: Controversy and learning. Review of Educational Research, 1979, 49, 51-70.

Johnson, D., Skon, L., & Johnson, R. Effects of cooperative, competitive, and individualistic conditions on children's problem-solving performance. American Educational Research Journal, 1980, 17, 83-93.

Kaplan, H. Increase in self-rejection as an antecedent of deviant responses. Journal of Youth and Adolescence, 1975, 4, 281-292.

Kaplan, H. Increase in self-rejection and continuing/discontinued deviant response. Journal of Youth and Adolescence, 1977, 6, 77-87.

Kohlberg, L., & Turiel, E. Moral development and moral education. In G. Lesser (Ed.), Psychology and Educational Practice. Glenview, Ill.: Scott Foresman, 1971, 410-465.

References

Laing, R. The politics of experience. New York: Ballentine Books, 1967.

Laing, R. Self and others. Baltimore; Penguin Books, 1971.

Lucito, L. Independence-conformity behavior as a function of intellect: Bright and dull children. Exceptional Children, 1964, 31, 5-13.

Madsen, M., & Conner, C. Cooperative and competitive behavior of retarded and nonretarded children of two ages, Child Development, 1973, 44, 175-178.

Maslow, A. "Higher" and "lower" needs. Journal of Psychology, 1948, 25, 433-436.

Merton, R. Social theory and social structure. Glencoe, Ill.; The Free Press, 1957.

Piaget, J., & Inhelder, B. The psychology of the child. New York; Basic Books, 1969.

Schmuck, R., & Schmuck, P. Group processes in the classroom. Dubuque, Iowa: Wm C. Brown Co., 1975.

Sites, P. Control: The basis of social order. New York Dunellan, 1973.

Stone, B. Relationship between creativity and classroom behavior. Psychology in the Schools, 1980, 17, 106-108.

Tittle, C. Sanction fear and the maintenance of social order. Social Forces, 1977, 55, 579-596.

Wallach, A., & Kogan, N. Modes of thinking in young children: A study of the creativity-intelligence, distinction. New York; Holt, Rinehart, & Winston 1965, 73-92.

Chapter Three

WORKING WITH DEVIANT GROUPS IN THE SCHOOL

Unifying Effects of Deviance

Deviant behavior is probably necessary to life, as noted in the first chapter. Consequently, everyone in every school probably participates in some form of deviant behavior. Educators and their students may deviate from social expectations in either their personal lives or in their professional lives or, most commonly in both their personal and professional lives.

Since most human activities are social activities which occur in the presence of at least one other person, most deviant behavior involves group participation; sociologically, two or more persons constitute a group. Deviant behavior necessarily entails the possibility of punishment and the need to avoid punishment often leads to the development of loyalty within the deviant group. Thus, students who truant from school may be be expected to "cover" for one another by writing parental excuse notes for one another. Students who get into fights on school property will often lie about their injuries to avoid suspension or expulsion from school; the student with a black eye, bleeding nose and bloody shirt will frequently tell the principal or vice principal that he "walked into a wall." Administrators may occasionally accompany one another to three martini "business" lunches; teachers may oversee other teachers' rooms so their colleages may take an unauthorized break.

Persons who band together on the basis of deviant behavior often have more intense group loyalties than do those who band together on the basis of conventional, or conforming, behavior. Those whose group loyalties are based on mutual participation in socially acceptable behaviors are not dependent on their group for social acceptance, safety, or continuing activity; these persons may easily move from one group to another since their activities are accepted by the larger society. The school more easily controls groups which have nothing to hide. Groups which engage in conforming behaviors are more open to regrouping and to external direction than are groups whose loyalties are based on deviant behavior.

Deviant groups often establish a subculture which has norms and values which differ from those of the larger group. Thus, students who fight in school are also more likely to smoke and to drink alcohol in school; teachers who take unauthorized breaks from class are less likely to prepare their lessons and to be on time for work. Deviant subcultural groups can create problems for the school in a number of ways. First, such groups often wield considerable power because of their intense loyalties and because of their fairly intimate associations with one another. These groups are able to work more co-operatively than are individuals or groups with less intense loyalties. Also, an organized gang, or deviant group, is often so tightly organized that it is able to discipline members who do not live up to group expectations; often, the deviant group is able to excercise disciplinary measures which are far more severe than anything available to the school. Thus, given the choice of following the group or of obeying the school authorities, the student may consistently choose the former out of fear of group reprisals which will endanger physical or mental well-being. Obviously, working with individual students will simply be ineffective under these circumstanaces; in such instances, educators must deal with the group as a whole.

Group Types

Young children generally play in what might be called "fluid groups," i.e., young children change playmates frequently and disciplinary problems tend to be those of individual children rather than of groups of children. Adults tend to belong to groups which are fairly "crystallized" in terms of consistency of membership, but complexities of adult life, e.g., raising families, earning a living, etc., require that adults belong to many groups and that they flow from one fairly crystallized group to another quite frequently. Adolescents tend to have group membership patterns which are more crystallized than those of adults, and certainly more crystallized than those of young children. Problems with "gangs" are problems associated primarily with adolescent youth; teachers often feel that discipline problems are worse in the upper grades than in the primary grades. Consequently, our main focus will be adolescent groups which create school disciplinary problems, though there will be implications for adult groups, as well.

34

Social groups appear to perform many important functions, among which may be included goal achievement, stress reduction, self-identity, and the realization of love and belonging needs. An understanding of the primary functions of group membership is essential for effective work with groups. The most common type of student group is one which is small and loosely organized; indeed, the small size of these groups really makes an organizational network unnecessary since simple face to face communication is usually available for the resolution of conflict and the formulation of plans. Individual love and belonging needs provide strong motivation for the establishment of these informal peer groups, which fulfill these needs by providing intimate person to person exchanges when necessary. These small groups also provide an opportunity for stress reduction through mutual support in the sharing of common experiences. For example, several adolescent girls who habitually ate lunch together were convinced that their families were pathological and they, themselves, perhaps bordered on psychosis. To illustrate her beliefs, one adolescent volunteered the information that she and her sister had gotten into a terrible fight while washing dishes in their parents' absence; in the course of this fight her sister had chased her around the house with a table knife and had actually thrown the knife just as she disappeared behind the bathroom door. Another girl in the group then volunteered the information that she and her sister had had a similar fight except that the table knife had hit her and she exposed a slight scar to prove her point. The third group member then told of a similar fight between herself and her brother, during which she was stabbed on the hand with a fork, but she had managed to reduce him to tears until their parents came home by smearing her bloody hand on her eye and claiming she had been blinded. At this point all three girls broke out in the relieved gales of laughter which are so typical of adolescent groups that engage in stress reduction and identity formation.

Groups may be very loosely organized, as in the case of a group of youngsters who simply "hand around" with one another; at the other end of the continuum, groups may be highly structured, as in student government associations, or as exemplified by highly organized delinquent gangs. The more loosely organized the group, the more appropriate it becomes for the educator to focus on the needs of the individual members

who comprise the group, which obviously satisfies some
of those needs. With very well organized groups, it
becomes necessary for the educator to focus on the
needs of the organization if positive changes are to
occur. For the purposes of this discussion, we shall
differentiate between informal groups versus formal
groups, which we shall call organizations. In this
discussion, organizations are formal groups which have
a structure that is independent of the individuals
that comprise the group. Thus, the school is an organization. If the teachers, the principals, or the
custodians resign, or are fired, the school will still
have positions for teachers, principals, and custodians waiting to be filled. The school becomes a self-
perpetuating entity by achieving an existence that is
independent of the individal members in the organization. Neither police officers nor social workers
have been particularly successful at eliminating delinquent gangs, for example. One reason for this may
be that most interventions are directed at changing
individual members, and this approach is ineffective
with organizations. The organized gang provides members with fellowship, fun, excitement, power, a sense
of enhanced identity, and with opportunities to make
big money. Working with individual members of the
gang will be no more effective in eliminating the gang
than would be the resignation of the principal in
eliminating the school. Further, if gang members are
to be swayed from gang membership, the alternatives
presented should fill the needs that are met by the
gang; many of those needs would be very difficult to
meet except through gang membership, though possible
alternatives will be discussed in sections that follow.

Informal Group Formation

Murray Bowen (1978), a well-known psychiatrist,
believes that:

> The basic building block of any emo-
> tional system is the triangle. In calm
> periods, two members of the triangle have a
> comfortable emotional alliance, and the
> third, in the unfavored "outsider" position,
> moves either toward winning the favor of one
> of the others or toward rejection, which may
> be planned as winning favor. In tension
> situations, the "outsider" is in the favored
> position and both of the emotionally overin-

volved ones will predictably make efforts to involve the third in the conflict. When tension increases, it will involve increasing outside members, the emotional circuits running on a series of interlocking emotional triangles.

(Bowen, 1978, pp. 160-161)

Although Bowen's primary concern is family therapy, much of what he says can also be applied to informal groups within the school. Specifically, Bowen suggests that over-dependence on others, or a state of ego-fusion, is characteristic of persons who "...are incapable of the 'differentiated I' (I am - I believe - I will do - I will not do) in their relationships with others. Their use of 'I' is confined to the narcissistic, 'I want - I am hurt - I want my rights,'" (Bowen, 1978, p. 162).

Many informal groups in the school, among students and educators alike, are comprised of persons who "hang around" each other in a symbiotic fashion because they are unable to stand alone, even when this is necessary to their own development as unique and self-sufficient individuals. Adolescents often have serious problems in knowing who they are. The changes in physical development and in social standing which are experienced by adolescents are as dramatic as the changes which occur from middle-age to old age, except that adolescents undergo these changes much more rapidly than do adults. Imagine, for example, being classified as typically middle-aged this year, with family responsibilities, youthful appearance, job responsibilities, robust health, etc., and two years hence being classified as elderly, retired, frail, separated from family, etc. These dramatic changes would be extremely stressful if they occurred over a period of two or three years, but this type of stress is probably equivalent to that experienced by adolescents in their dramatic growth from childhood to adolescence and to adulthood. Small wonder, then, that adolescents often need to establish an identity within a peer group by answering the question "who am I" based on the observation of "who are my peers."

When informally organized groups of youngsters create disciplinary problems for the school several options present themselves. First, the school may attempt to reduce either the size or the number of such groups. However, since educators generally view the socialization process as essential, and as even more "basic" than reading, writing, and arithmetic, the formation of informal groups is seen as a desirable educational outcome when the goals and values of such groups do not conflict with those of the school. Thus, the school might attempt to change the goals and values of disruptive groups within the school, or the school might attempt to influence group formation at the initial stages of group development, thereby avoiding the development of conflicting goals and values. Yet another option would be disbanding, or attempting to disband, the disruptive informal groups. Attempts at disbanding groups of youths who present disciplinary problems would probably compound those problems, however, and such attempts would either result in the groups going underground or in their becoming even more resistant to authority and more loyal to one another.

The path of least resistance for the school is that of influencing group formation at the initial stages. Indeed, schools do this quite consistently, but, unfortunately, it is usually done unconsciously and in an unplanned fashion. There is considerable reason to believe that grouping students according to ability level may often result in the grouping together of students who are failing and who may wish to rebel against the school and its attendant frustrations. Often, ability grouping is not intended, but this may be an outgrowth of scheduling. For example, if the "best" students take advanced algebra and the "worst" students take general math, it becomes more likely that even the gym class will be homogeneously grouped according to academic ability since having algebra first period makes it impossible, let us say, to have gym first period, and having general math last period makes it impossible to have gym that period. This is obviously an oversimplification of scheduling practices, but, particularly at the secondary level, students do tend to be grouped according to ability levels and they often find it necessary to form "hanging groups," i.e., groups of buddies who hang around together, in order to deal with the impersonalization which is often characteristic of secondary schools.

Since youth who are failing and frustrated often are grouped together by the school, this encourages the development of subcultural groups which are discontented with the school and with the larger society

38

which it represents. These dissatisfied and failing youth provide each other with mutual support in developing alternative goals and values which will wrench them from daily humiliations. These student groups establish goals, and the means to reach those goals, which will provide them with confirmation of themselves as persons who can control the environment rather than being victimized by that environment. Often, such youngsters will thumb their noses at the school by cutting classes, being truant, ignoring assignments and creating havoc in a attempt at reducing the stress they encounter as a result of being faced with chronic failure, a situation that very few adults could tolerate. Essentially, these youngsters refuse to play along with the conventional school games, at which they usually lose, and, instead, they create their own game, with its own rules. School authorities often see this as losers playing a losing game, but frustrated students often see rebellion as their only alternative in an otherwise masochistic situation.

Creating alternative schools, classes, and/or curricula will not necessarily lessen the frustrations these students experience. Riding a bicycle does not really compensate one for being unable to drive a car; the alternative of wearing high heeled boots to compensate for a short physique can be as humiliating as simply being short. Passing elementary math at the high school level is perhaps better than failing math, but it is not compensation for the inability to understand secondary math. Further, youngsters are often quite pragmatic and they often feel that schoolwork is a means to an end, that end being a well-paying and appealing job. Such younsters are aware of the fact that simply passing elementary math when one is in high school is not going to net a well-paying, pleasant job. If these youngsters must also look forward to a high probability of unemployment, regardless of their performance in school, as is often the case with black youth, then they are likely to institutionalize their subcultural goals and means by creating formal/ organizations, or gangs, to deal with what they perceive to be a fairly permanent problem.

Informal Group Interventions

Ideally, the school should help to enhance students' sense of self, their ability to differentiate themselves from others and to assume responsibility for their own self-direction. The school could contribute to this goal by acknowledging students as individuals, a topic which will be more closely examined in following chapters. Occasionally, simply acknowledging students by name will produce dramatic effects. An acquaintance of the author once found that the absenteeism rate for the center-city open school at which she worked was unacceptably high. Since the elementary students who attended that school moved about from one teacher to another for every subject, many of them felt that they were not really noticed as individuals. Then, each morning, teachers stood at the door and addressed each child by name and said, "Good morning," or something of the sort. When a student realized that teachers really noticed, and cared, whether he or she came to school, the attendance rate increased dramatically. Similarly, a student who feels important as an individual is less likely to require a hanging group to provide him with an identity; this type of student will be able to move freely from one group to another without undue anxiety. A student who feels important as an individual will want to make his or her own decisions rather than simply going along with the group. When individuals in a group insist on making their own decisions, it is less likely that the group will act irresponsibly.

However, as we have already noted, educators must usually work with groups of youngsters rather than with individuals; in this context, educators may often excercise considerable latitude not only in terms of teaching methods and content, but also in terms of grouping procedures. Glasser (1969) holds that the two most important human needs are the need for self-respect and the need to give and to receive love, with these two needs really being inter-dependent. Glasser also believes that success in school, as this is defined by the student himself, or herself, is crucial to self-respect in our society. Glasser suggests the use of group meetings as a way through which school can overcome the loneliness of failing students through getting them involved with each other and with educators by helping them find ways of succeeding and achieving self-respect. In these group meetings Glasser proposes that the therapist should help students make value judgments about why they are failing, form commitments for self-help, and either follow through with these commitments or endure the unpleasant consequences of not following through. Glasser sees the Reality Therapy process as one of problem solving and

40

the meetings he describes are invariably well-structured.

In using various types of informal group intervention it is important that educators develop sensitivity to the effects of grouping procedures, e.g., grouping all failing students together, but it is also important that educators channel the group dynamics by providing sufficient structure for informal groups. Psychoanalysts (Freud, 1921; LeBon, 1920; McDougall, 1920) have long recognized that individuals may easily regress to primitive, irrational, and impulsive states when placed in unstructured group situations. This phenomenon has been variously ascribed to the merging of the individual's identity with that of the group and as the substitution of the group for the maternal image (Fried, 1963; Money-Kyrle, 1950). Yet another explanation may be that the group represents an unknown entity to the new member, who may consequently experience great stress at being unable to predict what will happen to him within the group situation. If stress becomes sufficiently great, the individual's psychological defenses may break down and irrational behavior may occur. After a group has existed for a while, or once the group members come to know one another, the regressive group phenomenon is not so much of a problem because persons within the group form attachments or establish relationships which provide the group with structure; though the potential for regression remains, it is not as strong as when the group is in the formative stages.

Grouping procedures can sometimes facilitate the structuring process. It has been found that the best way to get youngsters to understand higher stages of moral development, as these were discussed in the preceding chapter, is to group together youngsters who differ only slightly in their levels of moral development (Kohlberg & Turiel, 1971), with the result that the higher functioning students will be able to get lower functioning students to "see the light" when moral dilemmas are discussed. Thus, grouping can be structured in a manner which will result in certain types of fairly predictable outcomes. When groups are organized with some consideration of probable group dynamics, based on the goals which have been established for the group, the regressive group phenomenon is less likely to occur and the group is more likely to be productive. Occasionally, for example, teachers will complain that a particular class

41

has been nothing but trouble all the way through the grades. Often, a disruptive class will consist of some unusual grouping of students, perhaps sixteen boys and four girls, for example; this class is likely to be difficult for the kindergarten and first grade teachers, but, if nothing is done to re-group the class, it is likely that a combination of bad habits, growing bodies, and pre- adolescent minds will create an impossible situation for the fifth and sixth grade teachers.

Often, it is impossible for the educator to influence group composition at the formative stages and it may then become necessary to work with already established informal groups. If these groups are disruptive or disinterested in school work, the educator must either attempt to destroy the groups, which, as was mentioned, is likely to be a losing battle, or the group, or individual group members, must be punished, which may increase group resistance by creating a martyr effect. Alternatively, the educator may attempt to change the goals and values of those groups.

Obviously, goals and values are established on the basis of perceived needs. The goals and values of formal groups, which will be discussed shortly, are more clearly defined and more firmly established then are the goals of informal, hanging, groups. Youths who hang around together often do so because it is convenient and preferable to being alone. Additionally, students may hang out together because they enjoy one another's company, have mutual interests and/or similar needs. Thus, the goals and values of informal groups tend to be of an intimate, or personal, nature. Educators who work with informal groups may often help these groups attain their needs for intimacy and companionship by providing legitimate and pleasurable opportunities for this. Many hanging groups would prefer a comfortable smoking lounge to smoking on the corner. Further, a school smoking lounge might provide interesting educational films for students to watch - perhaps films on smoking and cancer, for example! The smoking lounge, or a similar unit, could become a recruiting spot for various legitimate activities, such as a bowling league, a motorcycle or auto club, a comicbook collectors' organization, etc.

Schools often engage in a tug-of-war with rebellious students, which sometimes resembles a debate tournament, except that only one side of the debate is really listening at any given time. Commonly, rebellious students are told that if they are late, or truant, thus and such will be their punishment - period. Many students see this as a challenge to their autonomy and as further proof that the school is interested in its organizational regulations more than it is interested in them, as persons. Once this cycle has begun, it is very hard to break since each side, each opponent, at this point, perceives a win-all or lose-all situation. If schools perceived this conversion process as a courtship, rather than a battle, the process would probably be more effective. In a courtship, the courting side, if there is only one, is usually circumspect and careful not to offend. The schools have many power tools which are often not used. For example, peer recognition is an exceedingly powerful tool with adolescents. Some educators might shy away from a courtship model with rebellious students for fear of losing control over conforming students. However, conforming students could be awarded various types of recognition to which the rebellious students might be led to aspire, e.g., awards for perfect class attendance, or awards for promptness, etc. Traditionally, schools have seen their role as a paternalistic one, which involves teaching students that they must obey rules in this smaller society so that they will learn that they must also follow rules in the larger society, or else. The "or else" provision which is necessarily implied in demands for obediance or subservience is not working well in our nuclear society, where "or else" is too high a price for either side to pay. In a world which is becoming progressively more intimate in its physical and psychological relationships, where satellites can provide strategic information about any country to any country, where the citizens of many countries are in frequent communication with one another, and where the products of some countries are essential to the very survival of other countries, diplomacy, not obedience to authority, is the vital lesson to be learned. If students are to learn diplomacy, then the schools, themselves, must be models of diplomacy, rather than models of unyielding authority.

The parochial world of the past operated on black and white principles because relatively few comparisons were available; college students, a small social elite in the not very distant past, learned of dramatically different societies and social customs in anthropology classes, but the typical person led a

43

narrowly circumscribed life. The easy availability of inexpensive public media, world communication, and travel has made the relativity of social customs and behavior obvious to ordinary citizens. Consequently, "or else" social policies do not work on either the international scene, in the private sector, or in the area of criminal law, as the skyrocketing costs of prisons and the ever increasing numbers of prison inmates would indicate. Because socially imposed black and white models of behavior are no longer acceptable, individuals must be able to develop internal controls and coherent value systems which are consonant with reality, ego-enhancing, and attuned to the needs of other individuals and societies; methods of helping students develop these internal controls and value systems will be discussed in later chapters.

Formal Group Interventions

It will be remembered that, for the purpose of this discussion, formal groups were described as highly organized and as having positions, or roles, which are independent of the members of the organization. Thus, the organized gang usually has one or more formally asknowledged leaders; these leaders are filling roles which, were they to quit or disappear, would eventually have to be filled by others. Further, gang members often specialize in specific types of activities which, were they to quit or disappear, would have to be performed by others. Organized gangs are usually more of a problem outside the school then within the school; students do occasionally organize themselves into formal groups which may simply be protest groups, rather than gangs. Of course, most formal groups of students are sanctioned by the school, e.g., the student government organization, etc. When student, or faculty, groups are formally organized and seemingly in conflict with the goals and values of the school, a somewhat different approach is required to working with such groups than is the case with informal groups.

Formal groups exist primarily for the fulfillment of their goals and in testimony to their values. Consequently, while educators may work with individuals when dealing with informal groups, formal groups must be addressed by way of their goals and values since individual members of the group are usually either unable or unwilling to change the goals and values of the organized group. Individuals who disagree with the goals and values of an organized group are expected to leave, because these goals and values are the justification for the very existence of the group.

In many cases not all members of a formally organized group may be present within a given school. The values and goals of the group are given representation by those members who are in attendance and educators must clearly understand these goals and values if they are to work effectively with members of such groups. Educators should also be aware that "groupthink" (Janis, 1972) may result in poor judgment, particularly as regards an underestimation of the risks involved in the use of coercion. Since organized groups share a common ideology, meetings frequently create the impression that dissent is negligible and that the group, being obviously right as far as members are concerned, must surely possess might. A member who encourages moderation in the achievement of goals or in the use of coercive action may be seen as a type of Uncle Tom and may, consequently, lose credibility with the group. Since the adults in a school are more likely to be formally organized than are the students, the foregoing applies particularly to educators, themselves, who often expect coercion, e.g., the use of threats and punishment, to result in improved student behavior and attitudes; such educators often blissfully ignore the costs of coercion, e.g., hostility, destruction of the channels of communication, the organizing of maytyred individuals into yet more powerful martyred groups, etc.

Dealing effectively with organized groups often requires an ability to detect the hidden agenda behind the professed goals and values of the organization. For example, an organized group of educators may express a concern about school discipline which appears to stem from their concern with student achievement; however, most educators work in a very stressful environment and their concern with student discipline is often based on their own human need for a reduction of work-related stress. The astute administrator, who recognizes the hidden agenda behind the insistence on improved school discipline, will realize that disciplinary measures which may increase job related stress. e.g., larger detention halls or longer detention periods, will only increase rather than decrease teacher dissatisfaction, and if teacher stress continues to increase as a result of measures which actually improve student behavior, teachers may unconsciously

45

sabotage the new programs, as by giving detentions to too many or to too few students, or the teachers may raise new issues which again seem to be primarily related to their concern with academic achievement, as with an insistence on a greater number of special classes for students with behavioral disorders, but which are actually a reflection of their own human need for reduced stress. New issues and grievances will continue to erupt until the hidden agenda is addressed. Somewhat similarly, an adolescent gang may profess goals which are primarily territorial and power-oriented, but the hidden agenda may be a job substitute, i.e., activity which redeems one's ego while providing satisfactory income. Schools which are able to place their graduates in jobs which provide a satisfactory income may possibly avoid gangs which possess the forementioned covert goals and values.

It may often be possible to make a legitimate group more attractive than a deviant group. This approach is particularly effective if membership in the legitimate group makes simultaneous membership in the deviant group either difficult or impossible; the basketball player who must conform to expectations held for him by his coach, his team, and his fans in order to remain on the team is not likely to have the time or inclination to join an organized gang. Similarly, the teacher's concern with job security and his, or her, close personal ties with students from a wide variety of ethnic and racial groups may make membership in the Ku Klux Klan, or in the Nazi Party, considerably less viable than may be the case with someone who is either self-employed or unemployed. The more involved students and educators become in the affairs of the school, the less likely it is that they will establish membership in groups which have goals and values that are in contradiction with those of the school.

The school may often make membership in its own highly prized organizations too difficult; most schools have only one or two basketball teams, for example, even if the gym is not being used much of the time. A youth whose heart is set on being part of the basketball team may experience some serious ego problems when he is rejected because he is not among the "best". Educators would be appalled by the notion that only the best students should be given an education, yet, aside from infrequent gym classes, youths

46

who are not deemed the best in sports are not acknowledged as potential, or actual, team members and they
are often denied access to opportunities which might
further develop the skills they have while providing
them with a sense of self-worth and satisfaction.

Working with Mobs

Occasionally, students will group together as the
result of a particular event, or emotionally charged
situation, which is often the culmination of prior
social, or emotional, events. These groups are usually disorganized and they are often very volatile.
Obviously, the wise educator will make every attempt
to prevent mobs from surfacing in the first place.
Vestermark and Blauvelt (1978) suggest that the
schools control rumors, perhaps by having a rumor
control switchboard which students may call for the
"correct" information, in order to reduce the likelihood of major crises. Vestermark and Blauvelt note
that it is extremely important that an early warning
system exist, and that signs of possible disruptions
be heeded; if the crisis erupts, a firm but sympathetic approach may allow more effective communication
between the parties involved, but outside help, as
from the police department, may be necessary. Very
often, educators know of potentially volatile situations, but they ignore these in hopes that everything
will be okay, often because they simply don't know
what else to do. For example, in schools which have
significant numbers of individuals from different
minority groups, it is fairly usual for these minority
group members to associate almost exclusively with
those from the same minority group; this often happens
in the cafeterias of large corporations, as well.

Frequently, there is little communication between
the various minority groups in the school and individuals come to know those in other groups on the
basis of rumor and hearsay, and, generally, the rumors
are not flattering to the group being discussed. In
many cases, particular individuals would enjoy asso-
ciating with one or more of the other groups, but they
may be prevented from doing so because they fear
consequent rejection from their own group and because
the tight organization of the "other" groups leads
them to believe that they would be seen as intruders.
Teachers and administrators, as well as students,
experience the forementioned conflicts in schools
which have inadequate communication between various

47

cultural groups. Under these circumstances, a small incident between members of different minority groups can flare into a mob scene because rumors do accumulate and silent co-existence does build tension; therefore, what might otherwise be a soon forgotten fist fight between two hot-tempered bullies may turn into a major conflict between "rival" groups. Naturally, the surfacing of a mob is not predicated on the existence of differing cultural groups, but a "we" versus "they" attitude probably facilitates a mob mentality.

"We" versus "they" stratifications may be avoided with the assumption put forth by Marcus Foster (1971), a well-known school administrator:

> In trying to figure out what's going on, we can make the assumption that every-body is part of the system, even those who wish to change it. The immediate advantage of this assumption is that it legitimizes all the forces present. Our attention, thus, can focus on problems, not villains. We begin to see that there is a pattern of conflict - not a conspiracy - which is threatening to tear our society to pieces.

(p. 23)

Foster also points out that delays in acknowledging the just expectations of a particular group may result in rage, with a consequent expectation of justice plus interest on the part of the disfranchised group.

There is considerable evidence in the field of psychology that the existence of emotions, including feelings of anxiety, seem to enhance the probability of therapeutic change on the part of individual clients (Frank, 1974; Hoehn-Saric, et al., 1972; Luborsky, et al., 1971; Saltzman, et al., 1976). Somewhat similarly, Foster observes that:

> The peak of a crisis sometimes provides the best opportunity for beginning to set things right. For a brief instant, legitimate concerns may flash into the open. If one can perceive these issues, clarify them in the heat of battle, and harness the available energy, there is the chance for

48

turning a destructive situation into a period of reform.

(p. 40)

Obviously, it is best to identify the concerns of
groups, and the emotional currents which accompany
those concerns, prior to the emergence of a mob. Communication and sympathetic concern would appear to be
the key to the defusing of potentially dangerous situations. However, if a mob surfaces, an attempt might
be made at guiding this unbridled energy into productive channels - a difficult endeavor, indeed.

References

Bowen, M., *Family Therapy in Clinical Practice*. New York: Jason Aronson, 1978.

Foster, M., *Making Schools Work*. Philadelphia: The Westminster Press, 1971.

Frank, J. D., Therapeutic components of psychotherapy; A 25-year report of research. *Journal of Nervous and Mental Disease*, 1974.

Freud, S., Group psychology and the analysis of the ego. *Standard Edition*, 18, 67-143. London: Hogarth Press, 1959.

Fried, M., Grieving for a lost home. In L. J. Duhl (Ed.) *The Urban Condition*. New York: Basic Books, 1963, 151-171.

Glasser, W., *Schools Without Failure*. New York: Harper & Row, 1969.

Hoehn-Saric, R., Liberman, R. Imber, S. D., Stone, A. R., Frank, J.D., & Ribich, F.D. Arousal and attitude change in neurotic patients. *Archives of General Psychiatry*, 1972, 26, 51-56.

Janis, I., *Victims of Groupthink*. Boston: Houghton-Mifflin, 1972.

Kohlberg, L., & Turiel, E. Moral development and moral education. In G. Lesser (Ed.), *Psychology and Educational Practice*. Glenview, IL.: Scott, Foresman, 1971, 410-465.

Le Bon, L., *The Crowd: A Study of the Popular Mind*. London: Fisher Unwin, 1920.

Luborsky, L., Chandler, M., Auerbach, A., Cohen, J., & Bachrach, H. Factors influencing the outcome of psychotherapy: A review of quantitative research. *Psychological Bulletin*, 1971, 75, 145-185.

McDoughall, W., *The Group Mind*. New York: Putnam, 1920.

References

Money-Kyrle, R., Varieties of group formation. Psy-
    choanalysis and the Social Sciences, 2, 313-329.
    New York: International Universities Press,
    1950.

Saltzman, C., Luetgert, M., Roth, C., Creaser, J., &
    Howard, L. Formation of a therapeutic relation-
    ship: Experiences during the inital phase of psy-
    chotherapy as predictors of treatmnet duration
    and outcome. Journal of Consulting and Clinical
    Psychology, 1976, 44, 546-555.

Vestermark, S. & Blauvelt, P. Controlling Crime in
    the School. West Nyack, N.Y., Parker Publishing
    Company, 1978.

Chapter Four

ELIMINATING SCHOOL BEHAVIOR PROBLEMS

Although this chapter will provide educators with many practical approaches to discipline, while also providing an over-all theoretical typology for discipline problems, it is hoped that the reader will finish the chapter with the following question in mind, "Do I really want to eliminate behavior problems, or do I want to be able to cope with behavior problems?" Misbehavior in school is generally simply defined as disruptive or inappropriate behavior. However, misbehavior is extremely complex and it is desirable, though not necessary, to identify the etiology, or causes, of deviant behavior if appropriate measures are to be taken with the youngster who engages in such behavior.

In recent years, the emphasis on the science of behavior modification has led to a generally held attitude that if a child's behavior is the problem, then changing that behavior is the solution. However, experts who use operant conditioning, which involves the distribution of reward or punishment according to scientifically formulated schedules, sometimes become overly concerned with what is believed to be appropriate behavior, as defined by those in power, and they may lose sight of the real message behind that behavior. The reasoning which often leads to this breakdown in communication between the "actor" and the "modifier" is the fact that an understanding of the motivation behind specific behaviors is not usually necessary for the implementation of effective behavior change. For example, many of an infant's first vocalizations are often unpleasant. It might, no doubt, be possible to modify an infant's behavior so that he stops screaming and whining, regardless of his reasons for screaming and whining, with the very possible result that the infant might never babble or develop spoken language. But of course, no one would dream of modifying an infant's behavior in this fashion because much of child development is intuitively understood by even the poorly educated. However, much of human behavior is not understood.

Thomas Edison's school teacher sent Tommy home with a note to his mother telling her that Tom's brain was "addled", and that he was uneducable. Fortunately, Edison's mother was a teacher and she was able to

53

educate him at home. However, legend has it that
neither of Edison's parents really believed that he
was normal. For example, on one particular day, Tom
is said to have missed dinner, and his parents, concerned that it was getting dark and that he hadn't
returned home, wandered about the farm trying to find
him. They finally found him in the chicken coop where
he was sitting, ever so lightly, of course, on a
clutch of eggs. Now imagine your ten-year-old son
missing dinner to sit on some chicken eggs! Is this
disturbing behavior? For most parents, the answer is
definitely "Yes!" Is this also disturbed behavior?
Well, perhaps, but not if you are in the process of
inventing the incubator. Were Tom in elementary
school in 1982, he might well be placed in a classroom
for the emotionally disturbed. Indeed, it is frequently observed that many gifted children are placed
in such classes, some examples of which will be given
later. In a classroom for the emotionally disturbed,
or the behaviorally disordered (both terms are used
synonymously) Tom might be placed in a behavior modification program. In such a program, Tom might be
taught that his strange behaviors are upsetting to
most adults and to many children and that, for his own
benefit, he should do things as he is expected to do
them. We may be sure that not all of young Edison's
ideas were successful - for example, he might have sat
on chicken eggs and discovered that his hunch regarding the importance of heat for hatching was incorrect
- in which case his behavior might have been interpreted as "stupid" and "crazy". In a class for the
emotionally disturbed, Tom would be taught that if he
wants things that are important to him - such as
money, trinkets, free time, or some other reward that
he values, then he has to act "normal", as defined by
the teacher, the psychologist and the parents, or he
will be punished by being denied rewards which are
contingent upon appropriate behavior. Despite these
criticisms, behavior modification is sometimes the
most desirable approach to reduce deviant behaviors,
depending on the etiology of those behaviors, as we
shall see.

A problem which arises when educators concern
themselves with normal or average children is their
frequent lack of understanding of what is normal or
average. Most people are inclined to expect an
unrealistically high level of homogeneity between
"normal" youngsters. For example, many lay persons
and, alas, many educators, can be whipped into a

frenzy of concern when they are told that half of the
children in their schools are below average in reading. The average, of course, is merely a statistic,
not only for reading test scores, but also for behavior. We can mathematically identify what is average,
but it is often the case that no one gets the average
score.

Despite everything which has been said, there can
be no argument about the fact that some youngsters
engage in behaviors that are self-destructive and/or
dangerous or unpleasant for others. The teacher who
allows students to behave any way they wish is a
teacher who is unable to teach because of the pandemo-
nium in the class. An effective teacher must have
classroom control; this is not merely desirable, it is
absolutely necessary. How, then, does a teacher
establish control and, equally important, how does a
teacher decide which are desirable and which are undesirable behaviors? We shall now examine and discuss
a typology for school deviance which describes specific coping measures a teacher may use in dealing with
specific influences which may lead a student to engage
in deviant behavior.

Using a Typology for School Discipline

In keeping with the points which have been made
thus far in this book, it is important for the teacher
to select classroom control procedures which are consonant with the needs of particular students. Further, some school environments provide a climate in
which one approach to classroom control may flourish
while another approach may not. Hence, our concern
will be that only control techniques which are appropriate to particular situations and individuals should
be used.

FIGURE 2

Typology for School Discipline

Coping measures for	Influences to deviance
A. Narrowing boundaries	1. deviance as ego enhancing 2. deviance as fun and exciting 3. deviance as boundary testing 4. deviance as protest without expectation of change
B. Creating orderliness, meaningfulness and predictability	1. view of the world as chaotic 2. difficulty in understanding social interactions
C. Lowering tension and frustration	1. aggression as a result of frustration 2. deviance resulting from tension
D. Information and role taking	1. inability to understand reference group expectations 2. conflict of reference groups 3. cue misinterpretation
E. Behavior midification and/or covert verbalization	1. deviance as habit 2. limited behavioral repertoire
F. Acknowledging and respecting differences	1. deviance as as physiological condition 2. deviance as rebellion with the expectation of change 3. deviance as cultural difference 4. deviance as creativity 5. stereotyped deviance 6. deviance as personal choice

56

Narrowing Boundries

It seems ironic that narrowing the boundaries of acceptable behavior should result in greater conformity since the more narrow the boundaries of acceptable behavior may be, the greater the number of spoken and unspoken rules, or the stricter the rules. Logically speaking, a greater number of rules should result in more rule breaking since there are more rules to break. Similarly, stricter rules are more easily broken than more lenient rules and the deviant behavior should be more frequent under these circumstances. However, two social phenomena which we shall call the "margin of safety' and the "visibility of violation" help to bring about greater conformity, not lesser conformity, when the boundaries of acceptable behavior are narrowed.

Visibility of violation is a very simple concept but a very important one. Some rules make violations difficult to identify. For example, for many years, most of the lamp posts in New York City carried signs admonishing pedestrians to curb their dogs, but dog dung was everywhere - on the streets, on the sidewalks and under your shoes. The primary problem was that violations were not visible. If, for example, your dog littered the sidewalk, was it you or your dog who broke the rules? How close to the curb did your dog have to deliver his litter for you to have obeyed the "curb your dog" law? Then, the impossible happened, and despite the fact that the "curb your dog" law had bombed-out, a new law was passed which required owners to pick-up after their dogs! Well, said everyone, this will never work! If they won't curb their dogs, they certainly won't pick-up after them. But it did work! Dog owners all over New York City really did pick-up after their dogs. Why? No-one wants a parade of angry pedestrains yelling at one or a police officer following a hot trail, so to speak, and ticketing one for so humiliating an offense. So the new rule was stricter than the old rule, but it made violations more visible, and, in so doing, it increased conformity.

In the classroom situation, the teacher who expects complete silence and does not allow students to leave their seats creates a visibility of violation which does not exist in a more permissive environment. If students are allowed to talk, or walk around, passing judgement on abuses of these priviledges can be

57

complex; for example, how loud is too loud, which words or phrases can not be accepted, when is talking not permitted, and so forth.

When rules become so numerous, or complex, that they are not fully understood, a margin of safety is employed as a protective barrier, and this can lead to greater conformity until the importance of the rules is assessed. If the rules are strictly enforced, then the margin of safety creates an impetus for a further narrowing of the boundaries of acceptable behavior. An English speaking student who has had eight months of high school French often does not want to say anything in French class for fear of making mistakes and she uses monosyllables and short phrases even though she may know considerably more than this. A child who is active and talkative in most situations often becomes extremely inhibited in a new situation where the rules are unknown. New employees frequently follow all of their employer's rules religiously as a margin of safety against being fired. After employees learn how long term employees bend the rules, they often change their margin of safety in the direction of rule breaking, as with ninety minute lunches rather than sixty minute lunches, which may have been forty minute lunches for the first few weeks of work.

The automobile speed limit is an excellent example of the use of margins of safety. It is generally agreed that, partly due to limitations in the calibration of speedometers and radar instruments, traveling five miles above the speed limit is acceptable and many drivers habitually drive five to ten miles above the speed limit because they know that police officers overlook such minor violations. However, if the existing rules were to be strictly enforced, let's say that anyone driving 56 miles an hour or more was stopped for speeding, then the margin of safety would go in the opposite direction and most people would travel at less than 55 miles an hour even though 55 would still be the legal limit. Thus, depending on the strictness with which rules are enforced, schools may find students coming to school quite early to avoid detentions for lateness, or students may consistently come a few minutes late knowing that they are within a margin of safety.

The implications of the foregoing for school behavior are that not only should careful thought be given to the rules to be established, but equally careful thought should be given to the strictness or laxity of enforcement. Strict enforcement often means that the enforcers of the rules are seen as unreasonable, inflexible and unlikeable, but the effects of this enforcement will be that people, both young and old, will over-conform. If the rules are flexible, then the enforcers will often be viewed in a more positive light, but the margin of safety will be on the side of deviant behavior. If these observations are correct, it would seem desirable for schools to establish rules which are stricter than necessary but flexibly enforced. Financial institutions are already using this psychology in their loan programs - one's loan, or mortgage, payment is usually said to be "due" on the first or the fifteenth of each month, but one is usually given a ten to fifteen day grace period prior to being charged a late fee, rather than simply being told that the payment is really not "due" until a later date. Because of the grace period, debtors feel that at least they were given a "break" prior to being charged a penalty for late payment.

Narrowing the boundaries of acceptable behavior is particularly helpful in dealing with youngsters who have particular needs. For example, youngsters who believe themselves to be "bad" need to engage in rule breaking for ego-enhancement, or self-confirmation. We all engage in activities which confirm our own self-images. Harry, for example, defines himself as a "competent" person and he observes that he is good at math but poor at music; therefore, he describes math as his favorite subject and says he doesn't enjoy playing musical instruments; if Harry believed himself to be incompetent, he might prefer engaging in activities for which he has no aptitude.

Too often teachers believe that all children desire to be defined as "good." In actuality, we all simply wish to confirm the definition of self which most of us developed long before entering school. If one does not know who one is, one is insane. A view of the self which is consistent with environmental feedback and stable over time is essential to mental health. A young child who has often been told that he is "bad" generally comes to believe that he is indeed bad. Adults, on the other hand, can retain an image of self which is considerably independent of feedback from others because adults have had many previous experiences and they posses a "verbal cushion." Thus, if Harry is an adult who believes himself competent,

59

having a college instructor who tells him that he is incompetent will not be overly upsetting to Harry since Harry has had a prior history of competent activity and he is able to verbalize this to himself and to others.

The naive teacher who insists on telling a third grade boy that he is "good" when, indeed, he identifies himself as bad, may have the experience of one day saying, "Tom, you have been so <u>good</u> today!" Whereupon, Tom may promptly turn around and punch the child behind him in the face. Under these circumstances, it is necessary to make deviance as "easy" as possible by creating an environment where the boundaries of acceptable behavior are very narrow. Tom needs confirmation of his self-image as a "bad" boy, and, if the environment is permissive Tom will find it necessary to engage in a rule-breaking act which is quite serious. However, if the evironment provides many rules, Tom will find it quite easy to be bad. If one rule is that you must sit-up straight in your chair, all Tom has to do is slouch and he is comfortably bad. However, if the only rules in the class are that you respect property and person, Tom may find it necessary to hit someone or steal something in order to enhance his self-image. These practical suggestions for the teacher are not meant to obfuscate the fact that Tom should probably receive counseling and/or therapy. However, there are many individuals like Tom who are contributing members of society. The author knows an unorthodox lawyer who often accepts indigent clients and supports unpopular causes. This lawyer obtained his law degree on the basis of courses he took while serving time as a convicted criminal. This man has always defined himself as a tough SOB, and this definition of self probably contributed to his inclination for getting into trouble with the law just to prove how tough he really was. However, his self-definition as a tough SOB is now a prime factor in his outstanding success as a lawyer.

R.D. Laing, a well-know psychiatrist, summarizes the need for self-identity quite well, as indicated by the following:

'Identity' is that whereby one feels one is <u>the same</u>, in this place, this time as at that time and that place, past or future; it is that by which one is identified. I have the impression that most people tend or

60

come to feel that they are the same continuous beings through womb, to tomb. And that this 'identity', the more it is phantasy, is the more intensely defended.

(Laing, 1969, p. 86)

Thus, the child whose identity is that of a "bad kid", but who is insecure in this identity, is all the more likely to break as many rules as possible as often as possible to secure the self-identity which he feels is his, but of which he is not entirely convinced.

Some students like to lead spicy lives which are full of excitment. Breaking the rules is usually considerably more exciting than obeying the rules. First, breaking the rules carries the threat of punishment and this creates a highly charged and stimulating atmosphere in which the offender attempts to avoid detection and punishment. Also, breaking the rules is often fun. Most rules ultimately place limits on the things that many of us enjoy doing, else the rules wouldn't be necessary. For example, there are no rules which <u>require</u> sexual activity, though this is crucial to the human race, but there are many rules which prohibit such activity. Narrowing the boundaries of acceptable behavior is one technique which allows youngsters, and others, to experience the fun and excitement of rule breaking without actually causing harm to others. For example, let's examine two different classrooms. Classroom "A" is out of control, books are sailing through the air and desks are being over-turned; whereas, in classroom "B" students are quietly working at their desks. Students in classroom "A" would see a student who throws an eraser as "normal", but in class "B" such a student would appear strange and disturbed (and he might well be). Having "fun" in classroom "A" would require serious misbehavior, while a student in classroom "B" might have fun by softly mooing.

No matter how well defined rules may be, it is impossible to foresee all of the future circumstances to which the rules may or may not apply. When there is ambiguity about the applicability of particular rules, it often becomes necessary to test the boundaries of acceptable behavior in order to determine where these boundaries are. One of the primary functions of punishment is often that of informing those who have not yet broken the rules that certain types of behavior will not be tolerated. Again, the school related implications are that, since there will always be at least a few students who will test the outer limits of aceptable behavior, the outer limits of acceptable behavior should be somewhat narrower than really necessary, the sanctions employed in the enforcement of these limits should not be severe and, as mentioned earlier, the rules should be flexibly applied.

In schools where marihuana is being smoked in the wash rooms, beer cans being tossed out of the windows and youngsters being attacked in the halls, it might be asked "Where do we begin?" We probably couldn't even stop crime in our school if every corner of the school were bugged and all high school personnel were given roller skates." However, particularly with adolescents, and occasionally with younger children, peer group rule enforcement (and rule development) often proves highly effective. Vestermark and Blauvelt (1978) have suggested the involvement of student patrols and they have discussed the principles behind such patrols:

> ...students are the victims of criminal offenses more often than are teachers or other school staff members. It is generally their lunch money which is being extorted, and their person which is the target of the assailant's blows. Doesn't it seem reasonable, then to involve the victims or potential victims in the planning and implementing phases of a school security program? The key is to "involve" - not "use" - students ...
> Involvement suggests a forum where differences of opinion are discussed and where solutions have the consent of the majority.

(Vestermark & Blauvelt, 1978, p.289)

Imposing Order on Chaos

Youngsters with socio-emotional problems often perceive the world as chaotic, as not really making any sense. Frequently, these youngsters come from homes or neighborhoods were there is turmoil and conflict. Even young children know the way it's supposed to be, i.e., your mother is supposed to take care of you and you are supposed to love her, etc. Often

62

times, the most disturbing youngsters (but not the most disturbed youngsters) insist on having things somehow fall into place by acting out in protest against the chaos they perceive. Helen Keller, a brilliant deaf-blind woman, was completely uncontrollable as a child until her teacher, Ann Sullivan Macy, arrived on the scene, physically "tamed" her, and then helped her to make sense of the world.

A world which is chaotic is obviously not predictable. Therefore, when a child, or adolescent, perceives the world as chaotic, it is essential for the teacher to provide as much structure as possible so that the student has frequent opportunities to correctly predict what will happen next. The teacher can make the classroom orderly and predictable by using ceremony and ritual, by bracketing activities, by establishing well-defined rules and by organizing classroom space - each of these points will be discussed individually.

It is not by accident that many schools begin the school day with ceremony and ritual. Now that prayer in the schools has been declared unconstitutional, little remains except the salute to the flag or the national anthem, unless a school or classroom has produced its own ceremony or ritual. Ceremony and ritual are closely identified with that which is set apart, that which commands awe and respect, be it God, country, or some special cause. "Profane," in its Latin form, profanus, really means outside of the temple, and ritual, of course, generally occurs within the temple. Prior to entering the school building, childern come from a profane world, in every sense of that word. A first grade boy once told the author he wanted to be a school bus driver when he grew-up. On being asked why he wanted to drive a school bus, he said, "So I can yell 'sit down, shad up!'." When students enter the classroom, it is necessary to alert them to the fact that this environment is different, that it is set aside, that it commands respect. One way to do this is to provide ceremony and ritual. Ritual, by its very nature, is highly predictable: it is always the same, it is prescribed. In addition, ceremony and ritual is a social event in which one experiences membership in a group; it is also a no-fail experience, even if you don't know the words you can just mumble along with everyone else and you have successfully participated, this guarantee of success allows the participant to relax and unwind.

In order for the student's day to be meaningful and predictable, it is necessary for the teacher to organize time and activities. Older students should be given written schedules of activities which will be followed on a daily basis; younger children should be made aware of the existence of daily plan of activities and the same plan should be folowed every day so as to make the day as predictable as possible. In addition, the activities within the schedule should be bracketed so that changes are gradual. If a quiet activity, such as reading, starts the day, then the next activity should not be gym class. Quiet activities should be grouped together, and moderately active activities should follow, with the most active activities coming next, or this order could be reversed. The bracketing of activities facilitates the smooth flow of activities and eliminates some of the confusion which arises when the class must switch from one activity to another. The unstructured time between activities, when students are putting things away or taking them out, must be kept to a minimum if discipline problems are to be avoided. When the daily schedule must be changed because of unavoidable circumstances, the students should be reminded of what the schedule usually is so as to assure them that their predictions are sound. Further, changes should be gradually and calmly introduced, perhaps using the word "might" rather than "will" and giving the students a chance to mull over the change prior to implementing it.

When youngsters (or adults) feel that their world is chaotic, they know it is unpredictable and, consequently, out of control. People who feel that things are out of control see people and events as threatening and they try to control and manipulate others because one cannot trust a world which is out of control. The discipline problems which are created by disturbed students are often simply an attempt at manipulating and controlling the teacher. Most students are able to accept the teacher as an independent person who shows concern for students at times selected by the teacher, himself or herself. Disturbed students, on the other hand, want to control the expression of a teacher's concern and they will often misbehave in order to obtain attention from the teacher; they may also misbehave simply to anger the teacher, thereby proving to themselves that they have the teacher under control. By making the environment highly predictable, the teacher can help, such students to feel more comfortable and trusting in their relationships with others.

The teacher must also establish well-defined and anticipated limits. The students should know exactly what the rules are prior to these rules being enforced. If the teacher who sees a student chewing gum suddenly screams, "Throw that gum in the wastebasket," when nothing has been said about a classroom rule against chewing gum, the student may well interpret this as an indication of the teacher's dislike for the student.

Even if a student breaks a known rule, the teacher should not speak in a raised voice. A teacher's voice is a tool of the trade and it must be used judiciously. A raised voice creates excitement and results in a higher level of student activity, which is probably the opposite of what the teacher wants. A teacher's raised voice can also make a student a star by focusing other students' attention on him. Further, if the student does not obey directions which are given with a raised voice, the teacher has temporarily run out of ammunition and the student has won, at least until the detention slip is written. In order to avoid this, the teacher should reprimand with a very low voice; this creates at least the illusion of calmness on the teacher's part; it also does not make the offending student the center of attention, and it leaves the teacher some fireworks in reserve. Often, when the acting-out student is unable to hear the teacher's quiet reprimand, the student will yell, "What?" If the reprimand continues to be quietly spoken, the student's own voice will be lowered to a tone equal to the teacher's, and because he is curious about what the teacher is saying, the student may also drop his activity level so as to be able to hear - at which point it really no longer matters what the teacher was saying. If the soft voice doesn't work, and it usually will, there is always a scream waiting to be used.

Not only should the teacher's voice be subdued, but the environment should also be subdued and organized. A subdued environment may be necessary if behavior problems are frequent and serious; such an environment provides a minimum of noise. Lighting can also be used for rather dramatic effects on behavior. Every adult who has a favorite restaurant, or bar, has probably had the experience of arriving at the scene

before the evening rush and beginning an enjoyable
conversation with a friend; after a period of time,
the restaurant, or bar, becomes crowded, tension seems
to mount, individual conversations can not be heard
above the din of the crowd, and the evening seems on
the verge of being ruined. Then, the lights are dimmed, and dimmed further. Each time the lights are
dimmed the noise level is decreased as people begin to
speak ever more quietly, and the restaurant once again
becomes a relaxing place. The technique of subdued
lighting can also be used in the classroom.

With youngsters who have learning or behavioral
problems, it is often important to make space meaningful. Students should associate particular sections of
the school and the classroom with particular activities, for example, the reading corner is a comfortable
place where one is very quiet so that reading can
occur. Some children have difficulty handling large
spaces, which seem unstructured, chaotic and threatening to them. Consequently, it may be necessary for
the educator to break large spaces into smaller spaces
in order to avoid unnecessary behavior problems. Most
school lunch rooms are extremely chaotic. Not only is
lunch time a relatively unstructured time, but the
lunch rooms themselves tend to be large unstructured
spaces. Though children always seem to be entertained
by what adults generally consider to be disgusting
eating habits, the much more serious misbehaviors
which occur in school lunch rooms might be avoided if
smaller and more meaningful spaces were provided.

Lowering Tension and Frustration

Several suggestions for providing a subdued environment, which lowers tension, have already been
discussed. It is easy to see how an environment which
is perceived as chaotic and unpredictable would be
tension producing. Since many youngsters with behavioral problems also have learning problems, these students often encounter tension and frustration in their
academic work as well as in their encounters with
others. In addition to the previously discussed techniques of creating a subdued environment, organizing
space and creating a smooth flow between activities,
it is also possible for the teacher to lower classroom
tension by providing academic work which is appropriate and by using humor as often as possible.

Academic work which is too difficult for a stu-

66

dent creates tension by frustrating the youngster, and
it is well-known that frustration leads to aggression.
School work which is too easy for a student is often
interpreted as an insult to his/her intelligence, and,
sometimes, work which is actually at the student's
level is interpreted as an insult to his/her intelligence, and this also creates frustration. Therefore,
in order to keep the tension and frustration from
building up into aggressive confrontations, the teacher should be certain that the school work being required is neither too easy nor too difficult, and the
best judge of the appropriateness of the work is
usually the student, whose feelings about the assignments should be frequently discussed. Occasionally,
it will be necessary for the teacher to make the
assignment look respectable. An adolescent youngster
who has a math learning disability may require second
grade remedial work, but he/she will surely be humiliated by such work. However, second grade problems,
such as $9 + ? = 12$, can be transformed into high
school level work with a few strokes of the pen, e.g.,
$9 + a = 12$, $a = ?$

The human body seems to have several behaviors at
its disposal for the release of pent-up tension and
frustration, these behaviors include laughter, sexual
activity, weeping, fantasy, and agression. Of the
possible behaviors for the release of tension and
frustration one seems highly desirable, and that is
laughter. Some teachers are natural comedians and
they are able to lower tension in their classrooms
almost at will. However, even teachers who are not
talented comedians can create an environment in which
humor is likely to occur. An environment in which the
teacher is accepting of students' feelings is likely
to be one in which the students themselves will often
produce the needed humor. At a time when I was a
young teacher who was teaching a class of adolescents
labeled emotionally disturbed, I encountered a bright
and talented fourteen year old boy who was very insecure. Ben had requested that his desk be placed
adjacent to the teacher's desk; this proximity to the
teacher's desk resulted in a dramatic improvement in
Ben's behavior. Whereas Ben had formerly misbehaved
in order to assure himself of the teacher's attention
and concern, he was now able to feel that he was a
favored student because of the proximity of his desk
to the teacher's desk. However, I had, and still
have, the habit of standing in front of the instructor's desk when talking to students. One day, while

moderating a science discussion, I stood in front of my desk and forgot that Ben was left out of the group. Ben proceeded to put his feet up on his desk and to tap his ruler. Since the science discussion was proceeding very well, I didn't want to interrupt it and I simply attempted to screen Ben's behavior from the group by standing in front of his desk instead of in front of my own, and I took his ruler. Needless to say, this had little effect and Ben soon found other objects in his desk with which to play. The lesson continued to be interesting but Ben's behavior was getting increasingly annoying to me and, in a subconscious expression of hostility towards Ben, I invaded his personal space by sitting on his desk; whereupon, Ben said, "All right there now, Ms. Gagne, we all know that's your best side, but enough is enough!" The class thought this extremely funny and Ben had a very good laugh, himself. This laughter dissolved Ben's frustration and he thereafter began to contribute to the lesson. Obviously, however, this joke had been somewhat at the expense of the teacher and it might not have been made if the teacher's ready acceptance of such jokes had not been assured. Teachers who want students to help them dissolve classroom tensions through the use of humor should be aware of the fact that they may not approve of all the jokes which will be made, but only an accepting atmosphere will guarantee that jokes will be made at all.

Information and Role Taking

Students who misbehave sometimes simply don't understand what is expected because they don't comprehend how spoken and unspoken rules apply to their behaviors or because they misinterpret social interactions. Just as some students have learning problems in the area of reading, some students have learning problems in the area of social expectations; in fact, it is often those students with reading disabilities who also misperceive social expectations (Bachara, 1976; Bryan, 1977). In addition, poor readers often see themselves as inadequate persons and they are often hostile and aggressive (Andrews, 1971), and students who have negative self-attitudes are considerably more likely to commit deviant acts than are students who have positive self-concepts (Kaplan, 1977a; 1977b). Consequently, the educator must help this type of student understand social expectations by providing more detailed and more simplified information than is provided to the typical student; along with

68

this, the educator must help this type of student cope with negative self-attitudes, techniques for this will be discussed later in this chapter.

Just as some students need help in remedial reading, some students need help in interpreting social cues and in responding appropriately to those cues. Role playing and frank discussion should be provided for these students in a resource room situation where their special needs may be addressed without humiliating them before their more typical peers. Occasionally, the role playing should occur with youngsters who are average or above average in social intelligence. A student who has great difficulty in being accepted by others can often benefit from seeing how the most popular student in the class reacts when, in a role playing situation, she is placed in the role of a social isolate, or in the role of a scapegoat. If an astute student handles difficult problems particularly well, films might be made of her handling of such problems in role playing and these films might be used in helping socially disabled students model appropriate behaviors. Whenever possible these models should verbalize their reasons for acting as they do so that others will not only see the appropriate behavior but also understand why that behavior is appropriate. Since many youngsters with social disabilities also have related language and perceptual impairments, these problems must also be addressed. What, for example, is the visual difference between a smile and a frown. When someone smiles at you, does this mean he is laughing at you? What else can a smile mean? What are the signals that can help you understand how someone is feeling? Many students do not know how to give social compliments, which are such an important part of friendly social interactions. Some students do not know how to engage in "small talk". The forementioned social deficiencies are only a few of the many problems that students can encounter in their social adjustment. The remediation of social deficiencies should be as much a part of the school curriculum as is the remediation of reading deficiencies.

Some youngsters are simply unable to foresee the consequences of their acts or to deal with shades of gray in what they perceive to be a black and white world. For example, an industrial arts teacher once had an educable mentally handicapped youngster in his woodworking class who loved to fabricate stories. On

69

one particular day, this boy came into the shop and announced that he had found a twenty dollar bill on his front lawn. On seeing that the shop teacher wasn't paying attention to him, the boy added that he had taken the twenty dollar bill to the lost and found department at the police station. The shop teacher didn't believe this incredible story until the boy pulled out of his pocket a receipt which had been signed by a police sergeant and which said that if no one claimed the money within thirty days it could be claimed by the student. Though this student's actions were impeccably honest, his actions did not seem to be in his best interest, particularly since he also went about telling other less honest students about the incident! Too often, educators feel that their responsibility is to teach students what is "right" and what is "wrong". However, the world is almost never broken into right versus wrong. Ethics is a very complicated area of study and one in which too few educators are well-informed. How, for example, do we determine what is right when none of the choices with which we are faced is without pain and suffering for one or another group of individuals. Students need to be given many opportunities to imagine the possible versus the probable consequences of their acts. Not only should students be encouraged to imagine consequences of their acts, but they should also receive experience in verbalizing the various possible outcomes which may follow a given course of action, particularly as regards the effect of those actions on others. Television creates the impression that people are always in action and that reflection, planning, prediction of events and concern for others do not precede such actions; television actors appear to do things instinctively or impulsively, but not as a result of serious reflection or soul searching. The influence of television is substantial, especially in view of the fact that the average youngster watches television for an average of three and a half hours per day, or an average of 1278 hours per year (Barcus, 1973; Buss, 1977). If exposure time is used as a criterion, this makes television one and a half times more influential than school (Powell, 1971). Some students can verbalize only a few emotional states; for many, the only identifiable feelings are mad, happy and sad.

When educators attempt to place handicapped children in the "mainstream," or when they attempt to improve student behavior, they invariably focus upon the "students who have problems" and they expect these students to do the adjusting. This attitude greatly resembles what William Ryan (1971) has called "blaming the victim," which, at its extreme, is like saying, "What was Pearl Harbor doing in the Pacific," (Ryan, 1971, p.3). A more productive focus might be that of focusing attention on those students who are not experiencing physical or mental handicaps and social problems. How could the better adjusted, typical students help the more poorly adjusted students cope with the school environment?

There was a time when most youngsters were exposed to child development in the context of their own nuclear or extended families. However, as average family size continues to dramatically decrease, many youngsters really know little or nothing about children or adolescents who are not in their own age group. Most of these youngsters can be expected to grow-up and have one or more children of their own despite their overwhelming ignorance about the nature and needs of children. Probably no student in U.S. schools ever gets through school without at least some minimal exposure to biology, but psychology and sociology are almost never touched upon in school. Surely in a society as complex as ours, the emotional and cognitive needs of human beings, and particularly of children, must be given precedence over all other subject matter; but such is not the case, even as our prisons burst at the seams and as the arms race drains world resources. Principles of child development should not be a college level course. It should be taught from kindergarten through graduate school, and teachers should be teaching the principles of psychology and sociology at all grade levels, particularly in association with social studies and health classes, but also independently of these.

Ryan (1971) believes that "... the real function of the police ... is to keep order, not to enforce law" (p. 195). Unfortunately, as will be discussed in the following chapter, educators may see their function as the keeping of order in the gardens (or jungles) of education, while the avowed purpose of education is that of providing optimal opportunities for growth and self-fulfillment. The point which has hopefully been made is that not only do troublesome students need to be provided remedial help and information to overcome their social problems, but students who do not create problems also need to be made aware of the complexities of social problems both within

71

their own classrooms and in the world at large. More
will be said of this in the chapter which follows.

Some students have difficulty conforming to
school expectations not because of a social learning
disability, but because of a conflict in reference
group expectations. Although there are some basic
values that do seem to have universal appeal, most
social expectations are group specific. For example,
an Anglo teacher may complain that he is convinced
that a Puerto Rican child is a thief; when the grounds
for this belief are examined, it may be found that the
child did steal something on one or two occasions but,
more importantly, the teacher may complain that the
child will not look him in the eye when asked if he
took something. However, the Puerto Rican child's own
reference group might interpret his looking down at
the floor as an appropriate sign of deference to
authority and, if he looked the teacher in the eye, he
would be seen as impudent. Children, of course, have
no way of knowing about the differing expectations of
different reference groups. Since the United States
is a pluralistic society, the fact that multi-cultural
expectations exist must be explained to children. One
function of school integration should be a better understanding of the values which are held by various
cultural groups, but schools hardly ever educate students in regard to their differing value systems, perhaps because it is assumed that the WASP (White Anglo-
Saxon Protestant) middle class value system is the
"correct" one and that minorities should be embar-
rassed at not having those values. However, a more
likely reason may be that most people never really
examine their values and often are unaware of them.

Behavior Modification and/or Covert Verbalizations

Behavior modification is based on the learning
principle that a person who perceives that desirable
consequences follow a given behavior is likely to
repeat that behavior; behaviors which are followed by
punishment are likely to decrease. Many excellent
books on behavior modification are available for those
who wish a detailed treatment of this approach. A few
of these books are listed at the end of this chapter.

Behavior modification is particularly useful for
shaping new behaviors and for breaking undesirable
habits. However, strong advocates of behavior modification point out that consequences invariably follow

behaviors and that teachers who do not consciously employ behavior modification techniques necessarily employ these techniques unconsciously and, consequently, ineffectively. For example, the teacher who faces discipline problems may constantly reprimand students for their behavior and, in so doing, he may reinforce the misbehaviors, which will increase and continue because the students enjoy the attention they get from the teacher when they misbehave. The effective use of behavior modification usually involves rewarding desirable behaviors and ignoring, when possible, undesirable behaviors. With young children, or with youngsters who are severely handicapped, the teacher generally uses a primary reinforcer, such as food or drink. Older children generally exchange secondary reinforcers, such as check marks or tokens, for backup reinforcers, like trinkets, toys, free time, etc., which are usually chosen by the students themselves.

When a student has never successfully performed a desired behavior, it is sometimes necessary to at first reward any small behaviors which will eventually lead to the desired behavior; for example, if a seriously disturbed student has never sat at a school desk before, he might at first receive rewards for merely getting close to his desk, and then for touching his chair and, later, for sitting in his chair. At the beginning of the behavior modification program, it is usually necessary to reward a desired behavior everytime it occurs. However, it is important for the teacher to use intermittent reinforcement after the desired behavior has been established. Many adult workers get reinforcement for their work every two weeks in the form of a pay check. Since these workers get the check every two weeks, they make their work contingent on the fulfillment of a sometimes unwritten contract, i.e., getting a reward every two weeks. Consequently, if a two week period passes without their getting a pay check, they feel they have been cheated and they call the whole deal off - no pay, no work. Free lance writers sometimes write stories for which they have no guaranteed publisher and many of these stories are ultimately rejected, with the result that the writers are not paid for their work, but they will continue to write stories for quite a long time even if they are not paid because they know that they do sometimes get paid. Lottery games also rely on intermittent reinforcement for the maintenance of ticket buying behaviors. The teacher who wants students to work even when there are no rewards must use intermittent reinforcement and create students who are almost superstitious in their behaviors.

However, behavior modification is sometimes more difficult to use than one might expect, for he who modifies often, himself, becomes modified. A teacher of the author's acquaintance had an experience which led her to view behavior modification as an invention of Uncle Scrooge. This teacher had developed contracts with her students whereby she agreed to reward them for the performance of school tasks. At Christmas time, the teacher decided to give a Christmas party. The party included having the students make popcorn, but the students refused to make the popcorn unless the teacher rewarded them for doing so. In implementing behavior modification, it is important to carefully define the behavior under consideration; for example, if a porpoise has been trained to jump fifteen feet but the trainer is sloppy in his requirements and reinforces ten foot jumps, then soon the porpoise will never jump fifteen feet and may eventually not jump at all if it continues to get reinforced for progressively lower jumps. Similarly, if a teacher wants a child to sit in his seat, it is important for the teacher to define what is "in seat" behavior. One teacher meticulously defined "in seat" behavior as buttocks touching the chair; the students in her class quickly learned the principles of behavior modification and began walking around the room carefully holding their chairs to their bottoms.

Even the best known experts in behavior modification sometimes have serious problems with this approach, as the following will indicate:

> Aaron was ... a terror at bedtime - he refused to take his shower, threw temper tantrums, etc. We had painstakingly programmed reinforcement for more appropriate responses (e.g.,, with after-shower snacks) and consistently used the removal of privileges as negative consequences for transgressions .... Nevertheless, Aaron's rebellious patterns persisted. One night, I serendipitously said, "Aaron, do you want to take your shower in the upstairs or downstairs bathroom?" He stopped, smiled broadly, and said, "Downstairs!" His compliance surprised me (partly because he usually showered downstairs). ... Aaron's data were

impressively consistent - when we gave him a choice, he complied enthusiastically. When we did not, he counter-controlled. Several subsequent experiences added to my hunch that choice may be an important variable in the moderation of oppositional patterns. It is interesting to note that some of the most effective treatment programs for delinquency have incorporated substantial choice options - the delinquents have some say-so in their own contingency management.

(Fixsen, Phillips, & Wolf, 1973, p.37)

One can not but secretly admire those spirited beings who insist on exercising personal choice in their lives. Aaron's "oppositional patterns" may be moderated, but his victory remains clear.

Some of the more interesting approaches to behavior modification permit implementation by the students themselves. Students experiencing problems in their relationships with teachers, parents or peers have been taught to modify the behavior of those with whom they were experiencing problems (Gray, Graubard, & Rosenberg, 1974; Rosenberg & Graubard, 1975; Rosenberg, 1973). Thus, the most efficient way to employ behavior modification is often to teach problem students the principles of behavior modification so that they may interact with others in a more positive self-fulfilling manner; for example, if a teacher is suspicious and hostile towards a student who has a bad school reputation, the student might shape the teacher's behavior by sitting up straight, smiling, looking the teacher in the eye, and praising the teacher's positive interactions by saying things like, "When you explain things like that it really helps me a lot," and discouraging negative interactions by saying things like, "I can't concentrate very well when a teacher criticizes me."

Cognitive behavior modification includes the use of self-control training and self-monitoring. Children and adults have been taught to sub-vocalize self-commands such as, "I must think, look and listen before I answer" (Goodwin & Mahoney, 1975; Meichenbaum & Goodman, 1969, 1971; Palkes, et al., 1968, 1971). Impulsive children who use self-commands also need to learn what it is that they should think about before answering; teachers and peers have been used as models

75

who verbalize the appropriate logical thinking patterns which should precede responding.

A cognitive-behavior approach on which there has been considerable research is Rational Emotive Therapy, or RET (Ellis 1977), which is well summarized by the ABC design which follows:

A (Activating Experience). Your boss fires you from a job you would prefer to keep, saying, "I've had it! Your keep coming in late after I've warned you about this many times. And, in addition, you pay little attention to what you do while on the job, constantly daydream about other things, and do poor work. Enough!"
B (rational Belief). "I wish he hadn't done that! ... I've really put myself in a lousy position, and I foolishly got myself on the Unemployment rolls. What crummy behavior!"
aC (appropriate Consequence). Feelings of disappointment; strong determination to change your behavior in the future; displeasure.
iB (irrational Belief). "How awful that I behaved so stupidly! I can't stand my behavior! I should not have acted so foolishly when I had such a good job. And because I did what I should and must not have done, I can only see myself as a rotten person who will always keep acting this stupid way and who deserves nothing good in life!"
iC (inappropriate Consequence). Feelings of depression, despair, shame, and severe inadequacy, inertia and little inclination to overcome it or to seek new employment.
Having summarized the problem you can now go on to D (Disputing) like this:

My behaving quite badly or very badly on the job - assuming that I actually did behave that way when I had it - hardly means that I behaved totally badly. Most probably, I also behaved well or at least moderately well in some respects. I most likely did some good things while I held the job. And even the bad things that I did, I partly

76

did in the process of learning how to do
better. So if I got another equivalent job
and I learned by my mistakes on this last
one, I would presumably do decidedly or considerably better.

(Ellis, 1977, pp.22-23)

Using RET, adults and adolescents can be helped to
understand that some of their irrational beliefs
about events in their lives may be interferring with
their happiness and self-fulfillment. Younger children may need to employ somewhat different approaches.
Di Giuseppe (1977) gives the following example of the
use of RET with children:

John was a 12-year-old boy in a special
class who was referred for his continual
fighting with his brothers. ... John reported that his brothers were always making him
angry by calling him names. ... We then
role-played the situation with myself being
John and he playing the role of his brothers. He called me all the names his brothers called him. I would then say aloud,
"Just because they call me a name doesn't
make it true. It isn't nice to be called a
name but it's not so terrible and I can
stand it." The the roles were then reversed
and I called John the same names. He repeated the statements aloud and they were
faded over the next two sessions. At this
time John's parents reported that he was no
longer fighting with his brothers. John
later reported that since he had stopped
getting angry, his brothers had stopped name
calling.

(Di Giuseppe, 1977 p. 377)

Knaus (1977) has developed Rational Emotive Education
(REE), which is similar to the forementioned approach
of having a youngster identify the irrational beliefs
which lead to dysfunctional behaviors and having the
youngster use self-statements in order to bring his
behavior under control. Knaus reports using a game
called "mental karate" to teach youngsters how to keep
themselves from being upset by others' insults and by
their intolerance for their own imperfections as well
as the imperfections of others. REE helps children

77

become aware of the origins of feelings and helps them to discriminate between assumptions and fact.

There is evidence that when adolescents are given the responsibility of recording their own behaviors, the self-monitoring that occurs in the process of recording and graphing behaviors can have a beneficial effect on behavior (Broden, Hall & Mitts, 1971; Gottman & McFall, 1972; Polsgrove, 1977).

Acknowledging and Respecting Differences

Szasz (1963), in accordance with Reichenbach (1947), notes the following:

> Language has three main functions; to transmit information, to induce mood, and to promote action ... It should be emphasized that conceptual clarity is required only for the cognitive, or information-transmitting, use of language. Lack of clarity may be no handicap when language is used to influence people. Indeed, it might even be an advantage.
>
> (Szasz, 1963, p. 18)

Language is the primary tool of the schools; it is the medium of education, and students are the product. Unfortunately, teachers are often considered to be, and often consider themselves to be, those who "mold the minds" of children and, presumably, their behavior as well. So it is that this product, the student, is shaped by the tool of education, language. When language is used to impart information, the mind is not "molded" or shaped since information is neutral in nature, it is a presentation of facts and not a call to action. When language is used to induce mood or to promote action, the attempt is to influence or shape the thinking process. Certainly, a student who knows only the cold, hard facts and who is unable to see the emotional implications of those facts is one who can not be said to be well-educated; knowing that people are starving in India and not having any feelings about this "fact" is not a desirable educational outcome.

The outstanding artist, and even the outstanding scientist, experiences a reciprocity between himself and his product; excellence in art and in science

78

depends on a sensitivity to the materials which will comprise the final product and a willingness to find the right tools for the material, rather than shaping the material for the tools. Further, art, particularly, requires an openness to influences which are at once within oneself and without oneself; inspiration, in its original meaning, involves a breath of life from without which becomes an integral part of one's being.

The teacher should not be one who "molds"; the teacher should be one who holds communion. To commune is to share in an intimate fashion, to receive of another and to give of oneself. When discipline problems are the result of the mood inducing or action promoting uses of language, when they are the product of the perceiver rather than of the actor, when they are the result of the inappropriate application of expectations for conformity based on models of behavior which are overly subjective, then communion is the only appropriate approach, and only in and through communion can the subjectivity of behavior be understood.

The teacher in communion with a student stands as a totality, without fragmentation into social and occupational roles; true sharing requires a free giving, a mutual offer of wholeness in which each gives all and in which each reaps more than he has offered. Communion requires at least one person who is able to address the totality of his being to another and to receive the totality of the other's being in return. Communion requires a whole person, a person whose thoughts and emotions are so finely tuned that they are in harmony, so much in harmony that they are one; and it is this "oneness" that he who communes presents to another. Buber (1970) speaks of a similar phenomenon in the "I-Thou" relationship, which will be discussed in the chapter which follows. Communion results in growth, not in shaping or molding; but shaping and molding do occur in the schools.

The school shaping process includes a selective exposure to myths. Rollo May (1969) has observed that a myth is not characterized by truth or falsity, for example we may speak of the Christian myth without passing judgement on the validity of Christianity; rather, a myth is an attempt at explaining reality and making it meaningful; myths are generally created by artists and writers who record an objective or subjec-

tive reality in a meaningful way. Most religious
myths, for example, are an attempt at explaining why
we are born, why we live and why we die. Rollo May
believes that the conditions of our lives are changing
so rapidly that our myths are unable to keep pace with
these changes. The Horatio Alger stories of yore were
an American myth which explained the difference between the old world and the new, i.e., in the new
world it is hard work and honesty which determines
worldly success and not the social station of one's
parents. However, in a multi-cultural society such as
ours, Roots is a far more relevant myth for a large
segment of the U.S. population. The reality of a situation is a less important determinant of a student's
behaviors than is his interpretation of that reality,
and a student's interpretation of reality will be
largely determined by the myths which he employs in
explaining reality and making it meaningful. Only by
acknowledging and respecting the myths to which a student subscribes can a teacher correctly interpret behavior. However, the teacher should provide students
with exposure to alternative myths as a part of their
education, this has long been a function of the study
of literature and of bibliotherapy.

When deviance is a deep expression of a youngster's individuality, be it simply personal choice,
physiological characteristics, cultural difference, or
rebellion with the desire for change, a teacher must
acknowledge and respect this individuality if communication with this student is to be maintained; and a
teacher who can not communicate can not teach.

By its very nature creativity is deviant behavior
in that creative acts depart significantly from the
usual ways of thinking and acting. Some students are
creative in surmounting the emotional problems with
which they are faced. A teacher must always ask the
question, "Are my goals worth the pain I am inflict-
ing?" Demanding conforming behavior from students,
and causing them mental or physical discomfort, merely
so that more powerful others can feel comfortable in
what they consider to be strictly proper environment
can not be justified. True communion with students
would result in this approach being as painful to the
teacher as to the student, that is the crux of empathy. Further, the teacher who communes with students
will not stereotype a student by, for example, label-
ing him a troublemaker and interpreting all, or most,
of the student's actions as deviant. A teacher who

communes with students will be so in touch with a youngster's feelings that it will be possible to discern chivalrous actions, noble feelings, and genuine concern for others in even the worst "troublemakers".

References

Andrews, R. J. The self-concepts of good and poor readers. Slow Learning Child, 1971, 18, 160-166.

Bachara, G. Empathy in learning disabled children. Perceptual and Motor Skills, 1976, 43, 541-542.

Barcus, F. Concerned parents speak out on children's television. Educational Research Information Center, Microfiche # ED084860, 1973.

Broden, M., Hall, R.V., & Mitts, B. The effect of self-recording on the classroom behavior of two eighth-grade students. Journal of Applied Behavior Analysis, 1971, 4, 191-199.

Bryan, T. H. Comprehension of nonverbal communication. Journal of Learning Disabilities, 1977, 10, 8, 36-41.

Buber, M. I and Thou. New York: Charles Scribners, 1970.

Burr, P., & Burr, R. Product recognition and premium appeal. Journal of Communication, 1977, 27, 115-117.

Di Giuseppe, R. A. The Use of Behavior Modification to Establish Rational Self-Statements in Children. In A. Ellis & R. Grieger (Eds.) Handbook of Rational Emotive Therapy. New York: Springer Publishing, 1977.

Ellis, A. The Basic Clinical Theory. In A. Ellis & R. Grieger (Eds.) Handbook of Rational Emotive Therapy. New York: Springer Publishing, 1977.

Fixsen, D., Phillips, 'E., & Wolf, M. Achievement place: Experiments in self-government with pre-delinquents. Journal of Applied Behavior Analysis, 1973, 6, 31-47.

Goodwin, S. E., & Mahoney, M. Modification of aggression through modeling: An experimental probe. Journal of Behavior Therapy and Experimental Psychiatry, 1975, 6, 200-202.

References

Gottman, J., & McFall, R. Self-monitoring effects in a program for potential high school dropouts. Journal of Counsulting and Clinical Psychology. 1972, 39, 273-281.

Gray, F., Graubard, P. S., & Rosenberg, H. Little brother is changing you. Psychology Today, 1974 (March), 42-46.

Kaplan, H. Antecedents of deviant responses: Predicting from a general theory of deviant behavior. Journal of Youth and Adolescence. 1977, 6, 89-99. (a)

Kaplan, H. Increase in self-rejection and continuing/discontinued deviant responses. Journal of Youth and Adolescence, 1977, 6, 77-87. (b)

Knaus, W. Rational-Emotive Education. In A. Ellis & R. Grieger (Eds.) Handbook of Rational-Emotive Therapy. New York: Springer Publishing, 1977.

Laing, R. Self & Others. Baltimore: Penguin Books, 1969.

May, R. Myth is Modern Society. Lecture at Vanderbilt University, Nashville, Tenn., May 1969.

Meichenbaum, D., & Goodman, J. Reflection-impulsivity and verbal control of motor behavior. Child Development, 1969, 40, 785-797.

Palkes, H., Stewart M., & Freedman, J. Improvement in maze performance of hyperactive boys as a function of verbal training procedures. Journal of Special Education, 1971, 5, 337-342.

Palkes, H., Stewart, M., & Kahana, M. Porteus maze performance of hyperactive boys after training in self-directed commands. Child Development, 1968, 39, 817-826.

Polsgrove, L. Self-control: Methods for child training. Behavioral Disorders. 1979, 4, 116-130.

Reichenbach, H. Elements of Symbolic Logic. New York: MacMillan, 1947.

References

Rosenberg, H. On teaching the modification of employer and employee behavior. Teaching Exceptional
Children, 1973, 5, 140-142.

Rosenberg, H., & Graubard, P. Peer use of behavior
modification. Focus on Exceptional Children.
1975, 7, 1-10.

Ryan, V. Blaming the Victim. New York: Vintage
Books, 1971.

Suzler, B., & Mayer, G. Behavior Modification Procedures for School Personnel. Hinsdale, I1: Dry-
den Press, 1972.

Szasz, T. Law, Liberty, and Psychiatry. New York:
Collier Books, 1968.

Vestermark, S., & Blauvelt, P. Controlling Crime in
the School. West Nyack, N.Y.: Parker Publishing, 1978.

Chapter Five

SCHOOL JUSTICE AS FAIRNESS

School discipline performs a number of important functions. Disciplinary action, or the threat thereof, presumably discourages behaviors of which educators disapprove. Disciplinary action makes an example of offending students and re-establishes the limits of acceptable behavior. However, if school discipline is to be truly effective, it must appeal to students' sense of fairness. When school discipline is seen as unfair, students are likely to become more rebellious than ever. How, then, can the fairness of school disciplinary action be determined, what is "justice"? A well-known professor of law has made the following observations regarding justice:

JUSTICE IS THE ESSENTIAL VIRTUE of social institutions: It is a goal whose content is derived from the social values of a given society at a given time. Philosophically, it may be framed in absolute terms, but pragmatically it fluctuates in accordance to levels of social consciousness.

The idea of justice as an end means that each existing thing or thought seeks to achieve or attain the perfection it is capable of reaching or which is appropriate to its object. The ideal of law is to devise those rules and norms which are most likely to permit the attainment of the ideal of justice.

(Bassiouni, 1978, pp. 73, 75)

In contrast to the foregoing description of "justice", Bassiouni (1978) notes that, " ... the better law is that one which narrows the gap between interpersonal and social conflict and its just resolution, which is why 'fairness' is the more often sought after standard than 'justice'," (p. 74).

Thus, fairness may enhance the comfort level between the victim, if there is one involved, the transgressor, and society, in this case a micro-society, the school. Justice, on the other hand, would emphasize the best interests of all parties based on the type of self-actualization of which each is capable.

Obviously, it is considerably easier to measure comfort levels than it is to prognosticate self-actualization. Fairness is more likely to leave everyone feeling satisfied; justice may not be understood by those who are ignorant of the perfection which is appropriate to, and within the reach of, a given party. An understanding and an appreciation of justice may well require higher levels of social consciousness than does an understanding and appreciation of fairness.

An emphasis on fairness in the school situation may well result in outcomes which are very different from those which might result from an application of justice. For example, schools frequently fail to acknowledge personality conflicts between teachers and students; the assumption often appears to be that no "good" teacher would have a personality conflict with a student, and that this is an almost impossible occurrence in professional relationships. Despite the fact that both teachers and administrators are loath to admit to personality conflicts within the school and classroom, these certainly do occur. When there is a personality conflict between the teacher and a student, the conflict which ensues is usually a form of what William Ryan (1971) calls "Blaming the Victim," as in the question, "What was Pearl Harbor doing in the Pacific," (p. 3). If a student misbehaves and underachieves because of his inability to get along with the teacher, it is his (the student's) problem which is the focus of attention - not the unsatisfactory relationship with the teacher, whose superior verbal abilities and position of authority generally make it possible to elicit sympathy from powerful others. Consequently, if the teacher teaches the great majority of students in a competent manner, the student who is failing because he can't get along with the teacher is often likely to be retained for yet another year in that teacher's class. Adults who can't stand their supervisors always have the option of finding another job, or the hope of being fired; but children who can't stand their teachers are children who have "behavior problems," or who are emotionally disturbed. Since children are expected to be "socially mature," i.e., well-behaved, in order to be promoted to the next grade level, and since they are expected to achieve at expected levels academically in order to be promoted, it is "fair" to retain such a child and, though the retaining teacher will probably not be happy at the prospect of having this child for another year, the teacher will usually feel vindicated and pleased that the fact that the problem is the child's now seems properly evident to everyone. Justice, on the other hand, would require that the child's self-actualization, rather than the comfort of the school, be given prime consideration. If justice becomes the focus, the child may be promoted over the teacher's objections, or the child may be placed with another teacher mid-way through the school year, much to the teacher's chagrin.

Often, of course, it is the teacher who is the victim. The unruly child who physically abuses smaller children in the classroom may be physically brought under control by the teacher, and the child's parents may present themselves in the classroom the next day and berate and threaten the teacher in front of the entire classroom. If there are laws against corporal punishment in the classroom, it may be fair for the parents to do whatever they can to see to it that the laws are followed. However, justice would dictate that the teacher's control over the classroom is crucial if children are to learn anything at all and, consequently, parents who object to the teacher's disciplinary procedures should not embarrass the teacher before the class, nor should they deride the teacher in front of their own children, who are, after all, a part of the class which must be controlled. A just solution, therefore, would be a quiet conference with the teacher and/or the appropriate administrator. Obviously, the "just" solution would not leave the parents feeling as satisfied and as vindicated as the "fair" solution.

The foregoing discussion may leave the erroneous impression that "fairness" and "justice" are found in opposition to one another; this is not the case. Indeed, it will be seen that one of the most interesting and attractive philosophical views of justice is that of John Rawls (1971), in which Rawls advocates a "justice-as-fairness" approach. Therefore, justice and fairness can indeed be unified and such unification could result in dramatic changes in the greater society as well as in the school.

Conceptual Foundations for Justice

The most prevalent view of justice at the present time is that right conduct is ultimately determined by the usefulness of the consequences of that conduct and that the ultimate consequences to be sought are the greatest good, or happiness, for the greatest number. In the utilitarian ethics just described, "... the good is defined separately and prior to the right. The right then becomes that which maximizes the good - be it satisfaction, excellence, or whatever" (House, 1976, p.77). This view is very similar to the preceding discussion of fairness in that the comfort level of the majority is the primary concern, rather than the primary concern being each individual party, based on the type of self-actualization of which each party is capable.

A number of problems are evident with the application of utilitarian ethics. The most obvious problem is that the best interests of individuals, indeed, their very lives, may be sacrificed for the comfort of the majority. In deciding where something like an atomic energy power plant should be built, at least one consultant for the Environmental Protection Agency has suggested that, "... a big taxpayer would be valued more highly than a welfare mother" (Zeckhauser, 1976, p. 37). Though Zeckhauser notes that, "... net dollar contribution is a poor indicator of the valuation of the general society" (Zeckhauser, 1976, p. 37), he does insist that, "... it is important to identify ... expected quality and duration [of lives] should they be preserved" (Zeckhauser, 1976, p. 39). Indeed, cost-benefit analyses are generally an excellent example of utilitarian ethics. For example, when the federal government must decide which types of cancer research should receive the greatest funding, an important consideration is the benefit to be derived from that research; thus, lung cancer research receives more dollars than may research in many other areas because lung cancer frequently strikes middle-aged men who are supporting families, making contributions to society, paying taxes, etc. Research dollars spent on cancers which primarily strike the elderly would not yield as many benefits for the majority as might dollars spent on lung cancer. Somewhat similarly, auto makers may fail to fix faulty automobiles because the money they could expect to spend on repairs would exceed the money they could expect to lose in court from law suits for death or injury resulting from their defective product. A logical extension of utilitarian ethics would be that more money should be spent on educating the gifted student than on educating the typical or retarded student since the gifted pupil could be expected to show greater academic growth per tax dollar spent than could other students. Covert assumptions of this type of thinking include the probably fallacious view that a big taxpayer with a prestigious job makes a bigger contribution to society than does the poverty stricken individual who loves people and brings great happiness to those he knows.

Prior to the implementation of Public Law 94-142, the Education for All Handicapped Children Act of 1975, state laws generally required that children should be denied the priviledge of public school attendance if it could not be proven that they were benefiting from such attendance. Making school attendance a privilege, rather than a right, was seen as important for the welfare of the majority of the students, whose intellectual growth and psychological comfort could be adversely affected by the presence, and the financial expense, of children with serious intellectual, behavioral, or physical handicaps. Further, since little learning could be expected from severely or profoundly handicapped persons in institutions, despite a massive infusion of funds, these individuals were usually not provided with any type of training or education. Public Law 94-142 emphasizes the importance of the potential for self-actualization among even the most severely handicapped and it requires that all handicapped children be given an education which is appropriate to their needs regardless of cost. The emphasis on self-actualization regardless of costs to the general public fits in well with the description of "justice" earlier in this chapter, but it is at odds with the earlier description of "fairness". P. L. 94-142 is not consonant with utilitarian ethics, but it is in agreement with Rawls' "justice- as-fairness" approach, to which we shall now turn our attention.

Rawls' (1971) seminal work, A Theory of Justice, proposes that rather than that which is "good" being defined prior to that which is "right," the "right" should be defined prior to the "good," unlike utilitarian approaches, in which the greatest good for the majority justifies the means towards that end. Rawls' justice as fairness assumes that each individual has truly inalienable rights, to life and health, for example, but particularly to self-respect, which Rawls sees as the greatest, or most important, "good". Indeed, it is difficult to see how individuals whose lives are seen as less important, as evidenced by

nuclear power plants being built in their neighborhoods, for example, or as evidenced by their school
programs being inferior to those of other students,
could possess self-respect since the clear message
under these circumstances would be that they were less
important than, and inferior to, others. A person who
does not possess self-respect can not relate to others
in a satisfying manner nor can that person take satisfaction in achievement. The most frustrating students
that teachers encounter are those who appear to not
care whether they do well or poorly in school, or in
anything else; success or failure seems to be of no
significance to these students. A person who lacks a
well developed sense of "I-ness", or who is not satisfied with the self which is represented by that "I-
ness", i.e., who lacks self-respect, may ultimately
not care whether he lives or dies, as was the case
with the convicted murderer, Gary Gilmore. A child is
particularly vulnerable to his perceptions of others'
perceptions of him in developing a sense of "I-ness".
Gilmore (Schiller, 1977) observed that, "I seemed to
have a talent, or rather a knack, for making adults
look at me a little different, different from the way
they looked at other kids, like maybe bewildered, or
maybe repelled ... like adults aren't supposed to look
at kids. Beyond hate. Loathing" (p. 74). Also in
the interview which was conducted prior to the execu-
tion which Gilmore himself welcomed, was his observation that:

> I always kind of felt a victim of the
> "Fell" syndrome. ... It's from a 17th or
> 18th Century quotation. Its anonymous. It
> goes simply:
>> I do not like thee, Dr. Fell,
>> The reason why I cannot tell;
>> But this I know, and know full well,
>> I do not like thee, Dr. Fell.
> When I read that, I understood its meaning
> at once and applied it to myself. Nobody
> liked this guy, and they didn't know why,
> either.

(Schiller, 1977, p. 82)

In addition to being indifferent towards success and
failure in academic areas, youngsters who lack self-
respect often become indifferent to the morality or
immorality of their behaviors:

90

> They're [prison guards] charged with being honest, I'm not. It's their duty to be honest and fair. They aren't supposed to bum-rap me. It's my prerogative to fuck up if I want, 'cause I'm the crook.
>
> (Schiller, quoting Gilmore, 1977, p. 176)

The preceding is an example of deviance which has become ego enhancing, as discussed in a previous chapter. Youngsters who have developed a deviant self-identity perceive both a deeply rooted need and a fundamental right to assert this identity, to be themselves, to prove to others and themselves that they do know who they are, that they are sane and to be taken seriously, that they have "I-ness", be this "I-ness' ever so unsatisfactory to most people, and perhaps even to themselves.

Although methods of coping with youngsters who have deviant identities have been discussed in previous chapters, it is obviously desirable to avoid the development of such identities, which tend to be dysfunctional not only for the individual but also for the school and the greater society. Such identities probably develop quite early. Gilmore (Schiller, 1977) remembered that he already expected negative reactions from others at age eight; when several adults became extremely upset and angry at him he walked home singing and whistling to himself. Consequently, positive pre-school, or nursery school, experiences would probably be more important in helping children develop positive self- identities and self-esteem than would later school experiences.

Utilitarian ethics would condone the development of deviant identities in a few individuals if this resulted in greater happiness for the majority. The fact that criminals are usually permanently stigmatized ("ex-cons") probably indicates that a few such identities may benefit the greater society, else there might be ceremonies for removing the stigma. The consideration that one will be considered a criminal for forever may act as a deterrent to those considering crime, but it also loosens the social expectations for those who are seen as generally law-abiding. For example, every school has its "troublemakers" who usually take the heat, so to speak, for most of the trouble which occurs. The fact that teachers are watching Johnny and Bill closely because they are on

91

probation after having been caught selling drugs in the school means that the teachers do not have the time to watch Jim and Mary closely since they are not "suspects". As a result, the likelihood of Johnny and Bill being caught doing something "wrong" is increased while the likelihood of Mary and Bill being caught in a deviant act is decreased. Since a majority of youngsters do commit offenses which are sufficiently serious to get them adjudicated delinquent (Elliot & Voss, 1974; Marwell, 1966; Murphy, 1946; Porterfield, 1943) if they were caught, it is important to society that persons who are seen as typically law abiding, or as privileged by social class or social status, not be placed under surveillance which is so tight that the offenses committed by these typically law-abiding, or privileged, persons might be detected. Obviously, neither the school nor the greater society wants a majority of youth to be classified as delinquent.

Rawls justice-as-fairness approach would not tolerate the development of even a few deviant identities for the benefit, or comfort, of the majority. Rawls (1971) arrives at his theory of social justice by supposing an observer of human society who is both very wise and also well-informed. The observer observes human society prior to his becoming a part of that society and he is given the power to structure that society in anyway he wishes. This omniscient observer is ignorant of one very important thing, however, and that is the condition of his forthcoming human life; he knows not whether he will be rich or poor, sickly or healthy, bright or dull, happy or sad, loved or rejected, etc. Rawls then imagines the type of society such an observer would desire and he arrives at the following philosophical principles:

First Principle
Each person is to have an equal right to the most extensive system of equal basic liberties compatible with a similar system of liberty for all.

Second Principle
Social and economic inequalities are to be arranged so that they are both:
(a) to the benefit of the least advantaged, consistent with the just savings principle, and
(b) attached to offices and positions open to all under conditions of fair

92

equality of opportunity.

(Rawls, 1971, pp. 302-303)

If school disciplinary procedures were to be guided by Rawls' philosophical principles, a number of interesting developments might be expected. First, since Rawls sees self-respect as the most important of basic human rights (Rawls, 1971, p. 440), students would not be disciplined in a manner which would lower their self-respect, unless such punishment were in the interest of equal basic liberties for all, which is sometimes the case, as with the student who must be withdrawn from the classroom because of physical assaults on others. However, if the student's offense is simply that of not having done his homework, for example, his humiliation is simply an attempt at teaching him a lesson and not an attempt at ensuring others' basic liberties. Unfortunately, most disciplinary procedures do tend to lower students' self-respect, even when others' basic liberties are not at stake. The student who is given "internal suspension", i.e., who is made to sit in an administrative office rather than attending class, is usually exposed to raised eyebrows on the part of faculty and students alike; this humiliating "what's wrong with you" experience is part and parcel of the disciplinary action. In external suspension the student is told to remain home because he is not good enough to attend school, where he is obviously not wanted. Students who receive detentions are similarly humiliated, assuming that their self-identities are not those of confirmed deviants, in which case such disciplinary action may be a source of pride.

Students who have been humiliated in the course of a disciplinary measure may react in several ways: 1. they may become angry; 2. they may vow never to experience this humiliation again; 3. they may set out to prove that they can't be intimidated or scared into behaving properly; 4. they may feel that they have nothing to lose with future misbehaviors since they have proven to themselves that they can survive the worst humiliations the school has to offer. Students who are punished for deviant acts very commonly react with anger. Some of this anger may be directed at themselves for having been caught, but usually the students are well aware that most people get away with such acts most of the time and they feel unjustly treated by fate because they are among the unfortunate

few who have been caught. Such youngsters may give
vent to their anger by resolving to get away with it
next time. Obviously, the student who is not allowed
to attend class may experience, in addition to humiliation, disappointment at not being able to engage in a
favored activity, equally likely, though, the student
may feel relieved at not having to attend class. Of
the forementioned reactions to humiliation, only the
decision to avoid such humiliations in the future
appears to be rehabilitative, but since the resolution
may be to avoid the humiliation rather than to avoid
similar misbehaviors, even this outcome is of questionable value.

It seems ironic that schools spend considerably
more time and expense on unpleasant disciplinary procedures than in acknowledging and rewarding acceptable
behavior. Too often, many students are relegated to
the losers' corner; they never receive recognition for
anything since frequently the only recognition provided by the school is for academic achievement or excellence in sports. It would seem imperative that all
students be given an opportunity to receive recognition in some area of achievement. Sadly, the schools
completely ignore the existence of a wide spectrum of
very important abilities, such as the ability to empathize with others, the ability to make appropriate
moral decisions under conditions of stress, the ability to provide cheer and comfort to others, the ability
to function adequately in school despite great difficulties at home, etc. The preceding abilities are
neither acknowledged nor rewarded in the schools,
though they are certainly more important than most of
the abilities which are acknowledged and for which
awards are given.

In addition to an emphasis on the nurturing of
self-respect, an application of Rawls' theory of
social justice in the schools would result in a wide
latitude of permissible behaviors; dress codes and
hair length would not be disciplinary issues, for example, unless these interfered with the basic rights
of others, which is usually not the case. Yet another
important aspect of Rawls' theory is the emphasis on
any existing inequalities being to the advantage of
the least advantaged. Thus, using the guidelines pro-
posed by Rawls, academically retarded students would
be more likely to receive school awards than would
academically advanced students. Students with behavioral problems would be more likely to be recognized

for their appropriate behaviors than would youngsters
who are relatively problem free. Physically handicapped students would have more privileges and greater
acknowledgement of their achievements than would those
who excel in sports. At the beginning of this chapter, note was made of the fact that justice is a goal.
Often, goals are established so that human activities
are given a focal point; perfection is generally out
of human reach but the constant striving towards perfection is the moral compass which hopefully keeps
human intellect and emotions on the coherent path
which may result in genuine progress, rather than in
directionless technological, or social, change which
is of questionable value. Rawls's theory of social
justice may be criticized on the basis of its being
difficult to achieve, but the most valuable goals are
often those which are only approximated rather than
achieved. True progress consists of the journey
towards ever higher goals rather than in the attainment of any of those goals; this applies to school
disciplinary procedures as well as to any other areas
of human endeavor.

Method as Message in Discipline

Common sense and community expectations, as well
as the legal restrictions which will be discussed in a
later chapter, provide relatively narrow parameters
within which disciplinary actions must fall. For example, schools are expected to discipline students
without causing actual physical injury, which would
constitute child abuse; further, schools are expected
to discipline students in a manner which will not
create serious psychological harm. Obviously, then,
there are some fairly definite limits to the severity
of the punishment which schools may administer if they
are to avoid public outcries regarding their disciplinary procedures. Students are well aware of the con-
straints which have been placed upon educators, as any
teacher who has heard a student growl, "You can't
touch me," will testify; student awareness of their
"rights" provides further assurance that educators
will not overstep limits placed upon them. Since the
school has very little choice regarding the severity
of punishment, about the only choice left to it is the
type, or method, of punishment. It would seem that
certain covert messages may be given to students when
particular types of disciplinary procedures are used.

In the following chapter, historical considera-

tions will be discussed as these have affected the
view of the school, and of school discipline. The
covert, and overt, messages which the school wishes to
convey to students change as social conditions change.
As has already been mentioned relative to Public Law
94-142, there was a time, prior to the mid-1970's,
when school was a privilege, not a right. Those of us
who attended public schools prior to the mid-1970's
can surely remember at least one school assembly at
which the principal reminded everyone, and particularly the disruptive students, that school attendance was
a privilege and not a right. The many laws which now
regulate school policies regarding school admission,
suspension, and expulsion have resulted in school
attendance more closely resembling a right rather than
a privilege. Schooling can also be viewed in a number
of other ways; it can be perceived as duty, as democratic process, as inquiry, and as holistic, in addition to other possible views, such as "pain-in-the-
neck", which will be subsumed under the previously
mentioned views for the purposes of our discussion.

School-as-privilege

School may be perceived as a privilege under a
number of circumstances, including instances in which
access to the school is restricted and at the dis-
cretion of school authorities, or instances in which
the school provides reinforcement or punishment which
is contingent on student performance and under the
authority of the school. "Time out" procedures which
are sometimes used in behavior modification, involving
the removal of a student from the classroom and from
other socially reinforcing conditions immediately following misbehavior, implies that classroom attendance
is a privilege, as does expulsion, suspension, no recess, no gym, etc.

Educators are often delighted at the prospect
of getting youngsters to see school as a privilege
since this creates the appearance that educators,
themselves, must be cherished individuals. However,
the student may then deduce that, if school is a privilege, what the school does must not be very important to his life because if school were really important he would be made to attend. The student may also
reason that if school attendance is a privilege which
is dependent upon behavior, the school must be concerned with teaching academics rather than behavior,
and those who are "privileged," or important, are

96

those who excel in academics, not those who behave well; good behavior being merely a pre-requisite rather than a goal. If the school conveys the impression that students must behave in order to attend, period, then the student may be given the impression that acceptable behavior is, "No big deal unless you want to go to school, and who wants to go to school?" If acceptable bahavior were a "big deal", would not the school include this in the curriculum? If acceptable behavior were a "big deal", would it not be recognized at assemblies with trophies and fanfare? If the privilege of school attendance is the instruction of academics, and if he finds in academics only painful failure, the student may conclude that school is indeed a privilege for the "brains," but not for himself.

School-as-duty

Some disciplinary measures convey the message that school is basically onerous and that the disruptive student will be punished by being given a heavier burden of the unpleasant experiences which are embedded in school work. Students who are given homework assignments involving the repetitive writing of "I will not ..." sentences probably strengthen an already existing aversion to homework and to written assignments. Similarly, students who are given detention get the message that being in school is ultimately a punishment, but something that must be done.

Retaining a student in his grade placement for an additional year, usually with the same teacher, is sometimes seen as remedial rather than punitive, but little empirical research exists which would indicate that this promotes remediation in academic subject matter; in any case, the message to the student is that he has failed and that this dreadfully unpleasant and humiliating experience must be repeated. Occasionally, a student will find a way to salvage his ego despite his retention. One such youngster who was repeating third grade for the second time stood in the middle of class one day and announced, "Im king!" Since this child was taller and more physically mature than any of the other children in the class, it apparently seemed logical to them that he should be king. Thereafter, this child was accorded the usual rights of a king; everyone expected him to be the first to undertake a new activity, to be the first in line, to get the biggest piece of cake, etc. Usually, though, children who are retained feel that they are anything but the king of the class.

Corporal punishment also conveys the message that school is an unpleasant and humiliating place where duty must be performed if brute force is to be avoided. The use of corporal punishment may also result in youngsters coming to believe that brute force is the appropriate response when the stronger party feels offended or overwhelmed. It should not be surprising if the child who is fairly frequently given corporal punishment becomes a school bully; in being a bully, this child may feel he is practicing the philosophy which has guided the school in its disciplinary procedures. The child who is given corporal punishment is likely to feel humiliated and frustrated by this experience, and the likely response to frustration is aggression. Corporal punishment for a child is not unlike being gagged for an adult. Imagine yourself having an argument with your boss and being gagged as a result; if you can't vent your frustrations verbally, the next step is likely to be considerably more aggressive and less socially acceptable. The child who is spanked is often spanked because he has inappropriately expressed his frustrations, as by hitting another child, for example; if the child is spanked, he becomes even more frustrated and his next social, or anti-social, responses are likely to be even more inappropriate than were those for which he was spanked.

School-as-government

When the disciplinary action is mostly the prerogative of student councils, student patrols, and variously comprised committees, or when school rules are largely determined by groups in which there is student voice, be these groups sanctioned by the school, or be they pressure groups established by the students themselves, the school is likely to be viewed as a governmental body with a democratic flavor. Interestingly, in a recent visit to the Soviet Union, several school administrators told the author that their schools used student committees in determining what disciplinary action should be taken with student rule breakers; these administrators also noted that student administered discipline was usually more strict and severe than that which would ordinarily be given to students by the administrators themselves. One obvious advantage to the school when students are

98

given the authority to make and enforce rules is that it essentially lets the school "off the hook" as far as the students are concerned (parents may have a different view, of course). If students assume much of the responsibility for school discipline, rather than devoting herself to the control of vice, the Vice Principal might devote herself to other duties, smile at students, and perhaps even get smiles in return. Naturally, some socially mature and articulate adults need to serve on such student committees if the school is to fulfill its responsibilities, but the effectiveness of student input is often overlooked in disciplinary matters.

Active student participation in school discipline also has the advantage of preparing students for more effective participation in large and small social groups after leaving school. Students who feel that they have a voice in school rules are also more likely to obey those rules because, as a result of their active participation in drafting and in enforcing those rules, they understand and remember the rules and they also feel pressure from their peers for following the rules of which their peers have approved.

However, there are some disadvantages to student participation in school disciplinary matters. At least at the initial stages, the student groups are likely to be disorganized and relatively ineffective without a great deal of patient adult guidance. Invariably, at least a minority of students will be dissatisfied with the rules, the originators of the rules, and/or the enforcers of those rules. Further, students who take an active part in school disciplinary matters are likely to become active in other areas in which their participation has not been invited, as in school personnel decisions, or in cafeteria matters. Insecure administrators might have difficulty in coping with the overall student activism which might result when students become fully aware of the fact that they are real people who do have a certain amount of collective power.

School-as-inquiry

In some schools, asking intelligent questions is often seen as more desirable than having the right answers. In some such schools students may address their teachers on a first name basis since both teachers and students, alike, are seen as seekers after

99

truth and knowledge, with teachers acting as "guides on the side" rather than "sages on the stage". In this type of atmosphere "deviance" is somewhat more difficult to achieve since those who believe themselves to be engaged in a quest for truth and knowledge are less likely to form adverse moral or social judgements than are those who believe that they have the facts and know the truth. Of course, many of the youngsters who attend the mostly private schools which follow the school-as-inquiry approach come from economically advantaged homes which, in some cases, have been able to provide the child with the structure which may be missing at school; if the breakfast table conversation is at the level of the Wall Street Journal and the New York Times, the child may come to school with an already existing store of facts which makes the acquisition of factual material in school not as important as it might be to children from a different background.

Some obvious advantages of the school-as-inquiry approach in matters of discipline include the fact that since the world is constantly changing, particularly in terms of technology and social values, citizens must be able to adopt behavioral standards which are in harmony with prevailing social conditions at a given time and place. Experience with the methods of intellectual inquiry will probably facilitate adaptive behaviors in ever changing times. An understanding of the complexity, and perhaps the relativity, of knowledge and truth may help students in withholding judgement of the behaviors of others, thus making it possible for the student to better accept and understand those who might otherwise be rejected as deviants.

The foregoing assumes that students will grow in wisdom as a result of their experiences in scholarly inquiry. However, some students may decide that since there are no hard and fast answers one's behavior really makes no difference and Machiavellian attitudes may develop. Further, most of society operates on the assumption that there are hard and fast answers and the individual who is always ready to question rules, regulations and other social, moral, or intellectual assumptions, may, herself, become a social misfit, someone to whom others can not relate.

100

School-as-holistic-acceptance

Although the structure of the school may encourage certain perceptions on the part of some students, disciplinary and academic practices which are intended to implement particular philosophies, while also conveying particular impressions, will never result in all students perceiving the school as the faculty and administration may intend. Consequently, an understanding of students' perceptions of educators' perceptions and practices must be established in the process of communion, or mutual sharing of personal meanings, with the students themselves. In this context, the author is reminded of a scene in the movie entitled Ragtime. In that film there is a scene in which a young man who is being tried for murder sits at the defense table with his lawyers and occupies himself with cutting out paper dolls. The perception of the jury is that this young man is insane, but the young man's perception is that the trial is a farce and the cutting of paper dolls is his protest against the pseudo dignity of the court, as he perceives it.

Too often, schools make important decisions about students based on analytical descriptions of their behavior, e.g., "He proceeded to cut out paper dolls while being tried for murder." If the student is not really known to the great majority of the individuals who are serving on the committee which is making momentous decisions about this child's future, if no one on the committee has communed with this student, as is very often the case, it is likely that unwise decisions will be made with regard to this youngster's future; he might, for example, be mislabeled emotionally disturbed and placed in a special class where he may actually become disturbed as a result of his, to him, unfair and illogical treatment. On the other hand, youngsters who are fairly good at impression management, who sit quietly most of the time, for example, may get through school with no psychological services despite deeply rooted problems which may result in acts of surprising violence at a later time.

A major theme of this book has been the importance of understanding why a student engages in deviant behavior; yet another important theme of the book has been the importance of accepting the student as a whole person, who transcends the social roles he or she may fill. In determining why a student behaves in a given manner, an analytical problem solving approach

101

must be used which is heavily dependent on language, as analytical processes usually are. In accepting the student as a whole person, a holistic and nonverbal approach must be used. When words are applied to a person, it becomes impossible to appreciate the whole person on the basis of the language used because words are analytical they fragment reality while breaking reality into its component parts through a naming process. Holistic acceptance is largely a nonverbal process of the type which is found in the visual arts and in music.

Again, communion, or mutual participation, between individuals is required if the holistic process is to work, whether this communion be between the artist and the audience or between the educator and the student. If the school is to maintain effective communication with students, it is essential that students feel that they are accepted and appreciated holistically since no analytical process can be sufficiently comprehensive. In discussing music, for example, it is possible to discuss the instruments, the rhythm, the melody, the style, etc., but it is impossible to really know and appreciate the music being discussed until the music itself is heard. Music is considerably simpler than are persons. It should not be surprising, then, that no words can lead to true understanding of an individual, the whole person must be experienced if his or her behaviors are to be understood and if truly effective communication is to be established.

The interpersonal dynamics which are involved in the mutual experiencing, or communion, between individuals have not been examined by many writers. Martin Buber (1937) a professor of philosophy, wrote of what he called the "I-Thou" relationship; Buber's presentation of this complex subject tends to be complex and mystical in its approach:

> In the eyes of him who takes a stand in love, and gazes out of it, men are cut free from their entanglement in bustling activity.

> The moment of meeting.... At times it is like a light breath, at times like a wrestling-bout.... The man who emerges from the act of pure relation that so involves his being has now in his being something

102

more that has grown in him, of which he did not know before and whose origin he is not rightly able to indicate.

(Buber, 1937, pp. 15, 109)

Buber's treatment of the "I-Thou" relationship indicates that the "act of pure relation" often occurs when eyes meet, and usually lasts for only a short period of time; Buber notes that usually we relate to others in an "I-It" manner:

The world as experience belongs to the basic word I-It. The basic word I-You establishes the world of relation.

The human being to whom I say You I do not experience. But I stand in relation to him, in the sacred basic word. Only when I step out of this do I experience him again. Experience is remoteness from You.

(Buber, 1970, pp. 56, 59, 69)

The concept of communion, or mutual sharing, which has been introduced in this book is probably more comprehensive than Buber's I-Thou relationship, though at its highest level, communion does include the I-Thou act of pure relation. The advantage of the I-Thou act of relation is that one comes to feel the essence of another who, in turn, comes to know one's own inner self. In the school situation the I-Thou relationship is of incalculable value in making life more meaningful for the individuals involved. However, communion, as that word is used here, is sometimes [a process in which there is a very high level of conscious experiencing, during the course of which one comes to know the modus operandi of an individual, one becomes better able to predict this individual's reactions to a wide variety of situations because in the act of communion thoughts and emotions become so finely tuned that they are one, and so it is that the essence of the communion which is being experienced is highly informative in the mutual understanding of the individuals involved.]

Many daily acts of communion often occur between students and teachers because teaching, of necessity, involves a mutual sharing, though individuals who lack sufficient emotional maturity to have a well-

103

established sense of "I-ness" may not be able to share at the high level which is implied by the communion process. If one's thoughts and emotions are to be so finely tuned that they are one, one must, in a very real and deep sense, know who one is. An automobile can not be tuned-up properly unless the specifications of the individual components of the engine, carburetor, etc., are known. A person can not be in tune with himself unless he knows his own unique specifications, so to speak.

The teaching process most often resembles a projective test in which certain neutral stimuli are presented, e.g., "Death is spelled d-e-a-t-h." The usual face to face nature of the teaching process results in the teacher's perceiving many student reactions to a wide variety of such relatively neutral stimuli, and the student, in turn, perceives the teacher's reaction to her reaction, and the teacher sees the student's reaction to his reaction to her reaction, and so on. If at any time in the chain of events which, in this case, involves the perception of another's reactions, one of the perceivers relates to the other as a whole person who accepts the other holistically in this moment of personal revelation, then communion has occurred. The teacher, or student, who never accepts another holistically can never understand personal revelations; this person may learn facts about the other, or make observations about the other, e.g., "She looked sad when the word death was mentioned." However, the person who does not accept another holistically will probably make fewer personal observations about others than will the person who accepts others holistically at particular points in time. Further, a personal revelation can only be understood holistically since the depth and breadth implied in the concept of revelation requires a broader generalization when given certain specifics. The teacher who merely observes student reactions without partaking in those reactions can often describe what he has observed, but he does not have an understanding of the personal dynamics which operate within the student because he has not experienced the student's experience unless he has communed with the student by holistically accepting that student during the moment of verbal or nonverbal communication, which, under conditions of holistic acceptance, will become a moment of communion. In this situation the teacher not only observes sadness but the sadness that the student feels becomes the teacher's own, and only when the student's experience

104

is truly woven into the teacher's holistic being can the student be understood as a whole person. The problem is somewhat like that faced by a blind woman who wishes to know what the weather is like but has no one about to tell her whether it is warm or cold, sunny or cloudy, windy or calm, etc. The blind woman must expose herself to the weather in order to know it. Similarly, the teacher must engage in mutual personal revelation, or exposure, if he is to know his students at their deepest and highest levels, at those levels which transcend the student role and without which the student role becomes irrelevant play acting.

References

Bassiouni, M. C. Substantive Criminal Law. Springfield, IL: Charles C. Thomas, 1978.

Buber, M. I and Thou, R. G. Smith (Tr.). Edingurgh:
T & T Clark, 1937.

Buber, M. I and Thou, W. Kaufmann (Tr.). New York:
Charles Scribner's Sons, 1970.

Elliot, D. S., & Voss, H. L. Delinquency and Dropout.
Lexington, Mass.: D. C. Heath, 1974.

House, E. R. Justice in Evaluation. In G. V. Glass
(Ed.) Evaluation Studies Review Annual, Vol. 1.
Beverly Hills: Sage Publication, 1976.

Marwell, G. Adolescent powerlessness and delinquent
behavior. Social Problems, 1966, 35-47.

Murphy, F. J., Shirley, M. M., & Witmer, H. L. The
incidence of hidden delinquency. American Journal of Orthopsychiatry, 16, 1946, 686-696.

Porterfield, A. L. Delinquency and its outcome in
court and college. American Hournal of Sociology, 1943, 49, 199-208.

Rawls, J. A Theory of Justice. Cambridge, Mass.:
Balknop, 1971.

Ryan, W. Blaming the Victim. New York: Vintage
Books, 1971.

Schiller, L. Gary Gilmore. Playboy, 1977, 24,
69-186.

Zeckhauser, R. Procedures for Valuing Lives. In G.
V. Glass (Ed.) Evaluation Studies Review Annual,
Vol. I. Beverly Hills: Sage Publications,
1976.

Chapter Six

Legal and Social Considerations in School Discipline

The concept that juveniles have any rights at all is a fairly new idea. Plato and Aristotle conceived of both the son and the slave as possessions - and eighteenth century English common law, as well as the laws of the American colonies, regarded the child as a possession of its father, who had life or death decisions over the life of the child, a fairly universal attitude which is also found in the Old Testament. In the early twentieth century, it was not unusual for abused children to be protected by state laws which were written to protect domestic animals. The movement towards children's rights has no doubt obtained impetus and inspiration from similar movements for other minority groups. Additionally, the behavioral sciences have provided much empirical support for the contention that the early experiences of children may have irreversible effects on their future behaviors as adults.

The many state and local laws which govern the use of discipline in the schools are too numerous to mention; therefore, only federal laws and federal court decisions will be discussed in the present chapter. Historically, one of the most important legal concepts pertaining to school discipline has been the in loco parentis doctrine, which holds that the educator acts in the place of the parent in matters of school discipline:

> A parent may also delegate part of his parental authority, during his life, to the tutor or schoolmaster of his child; who is then in loco parentis, and has such a portion of the power of the parent, viz. that the restraint and correction, as may be necessary to answer the purposes for which he is employed.
>
> (Wm. Blackstone, Commentaries of the Laws of England, p. 453 [T. Cooley, ed. 1884])

Although some recent laws and court decisions have diluted the in loco parentis concepts of yore, the educator is still often expected to act in the place of the parent for all of the students in the

class or school in matters of school discipline, but
not in matters for which the teacher was not hired, as
in treating an injured finger (Guerrieri v. Tyson, 147
Pa. Super. 239, 24 A. 2d. 468 [1942]). Further, the
fact that the educator is resonsible for all of the
children in his charge means that he may, on occasion,
act against the best interests of one student, as by
turning him over to the police, in order to protect
other students. The depersonalization of the schools
which occurs in a highly mobile and industrialized
nation, where education is provided by specialists who
are often unknown, and sometimes unresponsive, to
parents may indicate that the in loco parentis doctrine is no longer really applicable:

> ... modern decisions involving school
> authority must be viewed in light of the
> cultural changes in the United States, which
> have produced different attitudes regarding
> the student's legal character. Totalitarian
> authority granted to the schools in earlier
> cases has given way to a new concept of stu-
> dent rights, and students have been recog-
> nized by the Supreme Court as "persons under
> our constitution." The natural consequence
> of this new approach is a clash between stu-
> dents' asserted constitutional rights and
> the in loco parentis doctrine....

(Bowdoin, 1974, p. 274)

Federal involvement in education

It will be remembered that any powers and responsibilities which are not specifically given to the
federal government in the U.S. Constitution were said
to be delegated to the states. Education is not mentioned in the U.S. Constitution and it should, therefore, be a prerogative of the state government. Indeed, this was essentially the case until the Brown
decision of 1954, which involved racial segregation,
and in which the Supreme Court reversed an earlier
Supreme Court ruling relative to racial segregation -
an unusual occurrence. In the Plessy v. Ferguson case
of 1896, a man who was "seven-eights Caucasian and one
eighth African" challenged the constitutionality of a
Louisiana law which required separate but equal train
accommodations for blacks and whites. Although the
Plessy v. Ferguson case did not pertain directly to
education, the Court did make mention of the separate

schools for blacks which had been established by Congress in Washington, D.C., and this "separate but equal" doctrine was largely accepted, except in the case of a few segregated colleges, until the Brown decision.

In the 1954 Brown decision, the Supreme Court determined that education was considerably more important in the mid-twentieth century than it had been in the late nineteenth century, at the time of the Plessy decision:

> Today, education is perhaps the most important function of state and local governments. Compulsory school attendance laws and the great expenditures for education both demonstrate our recognition of the importance of education to our democratic society. It is required in the performance of our most basic public responsibilities, even service in the armed forces. It is the very foundation of good citizenship. Today it is a principal instrument in awakening the child to cultural values, in preparing him for later professional training, and in helping him to adjust normally to his environment. In these days, it is doubtful that any child may reasonably be expected to succeed in life if he is denied the opportunity of an educatin. Such an opportunity, where the state has undertaken to provide it, is a right which must be made available to all on equal terms.
>
> (Brown v. Board of Education, 347 U.S. 493 [1954])

Thus, although the Fourteenth Amendment did not indicate that equal protection under state laws applied to students, the Supreme Court noted that the Fourteenth Amendment was adopted in 1868 and compulsory school attendance laws were not commonly in use by the states until 1918. In more recent years, the easy access to public media and the greater social and intellectual exposure which a more affluent society can provide have perhaps promoted an earlier social maturity which is reflected in the Twenty-sixth Amendment, ratified in 1971, which lowers the voting age from age 21 to age 18. The fact that youth must assume adult responsibilities at an earlier age than was previously the case has probably encouraged the filing of a greater number of court cases relative to the rights of students. Further, the courts have been more inclined to consider school matters as legally relevant in view of the fact that preparation for active citizenship is now an imminent responsibility of the school.

Historically, a very low priority has been given to the rights of minors. For example, the Kent case of 1966 was the first time the Supreme Court had reviewed a case from a juvenile court since the establishment of the first Children's Court in 1899 (Platt, 1977). The Kent decision was not far reaching, but it set the stage for the Gault decision, which was far reaching. The Gault decision was extremely important in determining that the interests of a minor are separate from those of the state, in other words, in establishing that a juvenile is a person who is entitled to procedural due process, a finding which is of enormous importance in matters of school discipline.

The details of the Gault case seem so outrageous that they will be oulined here in an attempt at illustrating the shoddy treatment which is often given to minors under the guise of protection. Gerald Gault was a fifteen-year-old boy who was arrested and placed in a detention home in the absence of his parents, who were at work, because a neighbor complained to the police that he had made an obscene phone call to her. The investigating probation officer did not report any of the facts of the case to the court; the report simply stated that Gerald was a delinquent minor. The juvenile court proceedings were not recorded in any way and the complaining neighbor was never present. As a result of this kangaroo court trial, Gerald was committed to the Arizona State Industrial School for the rest of his minority, which would have been six years since he was fifteen years old and majority was at that time reached at age twenty-one. An adult who had committed the same offense could have been fined fifty dollars or sentenced for no more than two months. Incredibly, Gerald's parents lost their appeals to higher courts and Gerald was placed in an institution for delinquents.

In 1967 the U.S. Supreme Court reversed the opinion of the Supreme Court of Arizona. The Gault decision conferred on juveniles nearly the same due process rights which are accorded adults, including the right to a timely and specific notice of the offenses

110

with which they are charged, the right to legal representation, the right to cross-examine witnesses, a
right to a record of the court proceedings, and so
forth. Later court cases, particularly the Dixon and
Lopez cases, which will be discussed shortly, extended
and clarified these rights for school disciplinary
hearings. Further, Public Law 94-142 has provided the
foregoing rights to handicapped students who are being
considered for special class placement. Since one
method of dealing with the disruptive student often
involves placement in a special class for socially
maladjusted or emotionally disturbed students, these
P. L. 94-142 due process rights are of great significance to the discussion of school disciplinary procedures.

Due Process in School Discipline

Since the courts necessarily deal with school
discipline problems on a case by case basis, it has
been, and probably will continue to be, impossible to
provide school administrators with hard and fast rules
relative to due process hearings in matters of school
discipline. The complexities involved became obvious
when one examines the range of possibilities; for example, how could a kindergarten "sit-in" be treated in
the same way as a college level sit-in? Consequently,
the federal courts have given the schools considerable
latitude in matters of due process, but in cases of
serious, or severe, disciplinary action, and particularly when the actual facts of the cases are disputed,
the student's due process rights are fairly well de-
lineated.

The courts perceive that the right to an education is protected by the Fourteenth Amendment, which
specifies that due process is required if a person is
to be deprived of life, liberty, or property. Federal
courts have variously seen education as a property
right or as a liberty. In the Goss v. Lopez case of
1975 the Supreme Court defined short term suspensions
as those which last for ten days or less and it specified the procedures to be followed in such cases:

> Students facing temporary suspension
> have interest qualifying for protection of
> the Due Process Clause, and due process
> requires, in connection with a suspension
> of 10 days or less, that the student be
> given oral or written notice of the charges

111

against him and, if he denies them, an explanation of the evidence the authorities
have and an opportunity to present his side
of the story. The clause requires at least
these rudimentary precautions against unfair
or mistaken findings of misconduct and arbitrary exclusion from school.

(<u>Goss</u> V. <u>Lopez</u>, 419 U.S. 565 [1975])

Long term suspensions required due process procedures
which are very similar to those specified in the previously mentioned <u>Gault</u> decision.

Even when due process requirements are followed,
however, the decision to suspend a student for offenses other than those which immediately endanger others
must be closely examined. Suspension provides immediate temporary relief for school personnel and, sometimes, for other students, as well. The disadvantages
of suspension may outweigh the advantages in the long
run, as the following excerpt from a report by the
Chidren's Defense Fund (1974) indicates:

> While precise measurement of the psy-
> chological and educational harm done by a
> suspension is impossible, it is clear that
> any exclusion from school interrupts the
> child's educational process and forcibly
> removes the child from his normal daily en-
> vironment. It is not clear what good such
> punishment does. In fact, it may work
> against the child's improvement in at least
> four ways. First, it forbids the child from
> participating in academic work. If children
> with discipline problems also are weak in
> their studies, their missed classes, assign-
> ments and exams may doom them to fail com-
> pletely. Second, suspensions merely remove
> troubling children. They do not set in
> motion diagnostic or supportive services
> that might uncover and remediate the causes
> of a child's behavior. Thus, suspensions
> deny help to children. Third, suspension
> is a powerful label that not only stigmat-
> izes a child while in school (or out of
> it), but follows the child beyond school to
> later academic or employment pursuits. And
> fourth, suspensions are highly correlated
> with juvenile delinquency. Putting children

out of school, leaving them idle with no supervision, expecially when they are demonstrating they have problems, leaves children alone to cope with their future.

(p.135)

An additional problem not mentioned in the preceding involves the attitude some failing and disruptive students have developed towards school. Often, such students have had so many unpleasant experiences in school that they have become negatively conditioned to school. For students such as these, suspension may mean unexpected holidays; not having to attend school may be source of relief, if not of joy. Expulsions are not the prerogative of the school principal; expulsions are within the domain of the school board and require formal hearings.

Corporal punishment

In Ingraham v. Wright, 97 S. Ct. 1401 (1977) the Supreme Court ruled that corporal punishment is not cruel and unusual punishment, as this is described in the eighth Amendment. Ingraham v. Wright involved the severe paddling of two students, one of whom was paddled because he was slow in responding to a teacher's instructions. In that decision the Court ruled that the due process provisions of prior notice and a hearing do not apply to corporal punishment, but the court assumed that the disciplinarian would investigate prior to administering punishment if a student denied the offense. Although there are no laws forbidding corporal punishment at the federal level, many states and/or local school boards forbid the use of corporal punishment.

In instances where corporal punishment is not against state or local laws, the Baker decision of 1975, which was upheld by the Supreme Court in 1976, determined that the parents may not enjoin the use of corporal punishment for their own children. Further, the Baker case determined that although neither prior notice, in the due process sense of that term, nor a hearing, is required prior to the administration of corporal punishment, certain steps should be followed in the use of such disciplinary action:

(a) Except for those acts of misconduct which are so antisocial or disruptive in

113

nature as to shock the conscience, corporal punishment may never be used unless the student was informed beforehand that specific misbehavior could occasion its use, and, subject to this exception, it should never be employed as a first line of punishment for misbehavior. The requirements of an announced possibility of corporal punishment and an attempt to modify behavior by some other means - keeping after school, assigning extra work, or some other punishment - will insure that the child has clear notice that certain behavior subjects him to physical punishment.

(b) A teacher or principal may punish corporally only in the presence of a second school official (teacher or principal), who must be informed beforehand and in the student's presence of the reason for the punishment. The student need not be afforded a formal opportunity to present his side to the second official; this requirement is intended only to allow a student to protest, spontaneously, an egregiously arbitrary or contrived application of punishment.

(c) An official who has administered such punishment must provide the child's parent, upon request, a written explanation of his reasons and the name of the second official who was present.

(Baker v. Owen, 395 F. Supp. 294 [M.D. N.C.] [1975])

School Discipline and Individual Rights

In the famous Tinker decision of 1969, the Supreme Court ruled that students are not stripped of their constitutional rights at the schoolhouse gate. Prior to the Tinker decision schools had been allowed to enforce almost any rules which could reasonably be shown to promote school discipline - not a difficult task for educators. Although the Tinker case involved the expulsion of students for wearing black armbands in protest against the Vietnam war, the Supreme Court decision in that case has been unimaginably far reaching in the establishment of student rights and, by implication, in the restriction of school discipline.

School officials involved in the Tinker case held that
the wearing of armbands in protest against the Vietnam
war was disruptive to school discipline because many
students supported the war. The Supreme Court noted
that students were entitled to symbolic free speech in
the wearing of armbands just as other students were
allowed to wear political campaign buttons. The Court
held that the wearing of armbands did not materially
disrupt school work or interfere with the rights of
others.

The free speech rights of students, as outlined
in the Tinker case, have been extended to student
newspapers, over which the schools have little control:

> Under the First Amendment and its deci-
> sional explication, we conclude that: 1) ex-
> pression by high school students can be pro-
> hibited altogether if it materially and sub-
> stantially interferes with school activities
> or with the rights of other students of
> teachers, or if the school administration
> can demonstrate reasonable cause to believe
> that the expression would engender such
> material and substantial interference; 2)
> expression by high school students cannot be
> prohibited solely because other students,
> teachers, administrators, or parents may
> disagree with its content; 3) efforts at ex-
> pression by high school students may be sub-
> jected to prior screening under clear and
> reasonable regulations; and 4) expression by
> high school students may be limited in man-
> ner, place, or time by means of reasonable
> and equally applied regulations.
>
> (Shanley v. Northeast Independent
> School District, 462 F. 2d. 960 [1972])

The Supreme Court has consistently refused to hear
cases pertaining to dress codes and hair styles.
Lower courts have been about evenly divided over
whether hair styles and dress are symbolic speech,
which is a freedom protected by the Constitution, as
in the wearing of armbands. About half of the lower
federal courts have ruled that hair styles and dress
codes are matters over which the school authorities
have jurisdiction.

Students' desks and lockers actually belong to

the school, which is represented by the principal, and she may search these, or cause them to be searched, when this is in the best interest of the school, or when the lockers appear to be used for illicit purposes (People v. Overton, 229 N. E. 2d. 596, 20 N.Y. 2d. 360 [1967]; State of Kansas v. Stein, 456 P.2d. 1, 203 Kan. 638 [1969]). Further, in keeping with the in loco parentis doctrine, a principal may search, or cause to be searched, a student and/or the student's private property if the principal is not acting in cooperation with the police or other legal agency, and if the principal reasonably suspects the student to be guilty of an offense (People v. Jackson 319 N.Y. 2d. 731 [1971]; State v. Baccino 282A. 2d. 869 [1971]).

The courts have generally ruled that the disciplinary measures which are employed against students should reflect the educational goals of the school. For example, students may not be barred from graduation exercises because of misbehaviors which have nothing to do with their qualifications to graduate. A case in point is Ladson v. Board of Education, Union Free School District #9, 323 N.Y.S. 2d 545 (Sup. Ct. 1971) which involved a senior black girl who allegedly assaulted the high school principal during a stoning incident between blacks and whites:

> The Court is persuaded that punishment and discipline should be responsive to the educational goals to which the school system is dedicated. Courts are dedicated not only to the administration of laws, but to the pursuit of justice, and the two ideals must come together. The justice of the situation favors graduation attendance. We have here a student of demonstrated dedication, who has persevered through all of her term in high school and has completed her final year under adversity, even though some of that adversity may be of her own doing. She has been accepted at college. Her graduation ceremony is important and meaningful to her personally and in her family which has never before had a high school graduate. She has no other record of school disorder than the one incident here involved. It would indeed be a distortion of our educational process in this period of youthful discontentment to snatch from a young woman at the point of educational fruition the savoring of her ed-

ucational success. The Court believes that
not to be a reasonable punishment meant to
encourage the best educational results.

(Id. at 550)

Similarly, since the barring of married students from
extracurricula activities cannot be shown to reflect
the educational goals of the school, such students
must be allowed to participate in extracurricula activities:

> ... The Lone Oak Independent School
> District sets up a classification of indi-
> viduals to be treated differently from the
> remainder of the school students without
> being designed to promote a compelling state
> interest.... Appellees have not shown a
> clear and present danger to the other stu-
> dent's physical and emotional safety and
> well-being, or any other danger to the other
> students, faculty, or school property, nor
> any substantial or material danger to the
> operation of the public schools by allowing
> married students to participate in athlet-
> ics. The burden of proof is upon the school
> district to show that its rule should be
> upheld as a necessary restraint to promote a
> compelling state interest.
> It is the public policy of this state
> to encourage marriage rather than living
> together unmarried. To promote that public
> policy, we have sanctioned by statute the
> marriage ceremony .... It therefore seems
> illogical to say that a school district can
> make a rule punishing a student for entering
> into a status authorized and sanctioned by
> the laws of this state. We find no logical
> bases for such rule.

(Bell v. Lone Oak Independent School
District, 507 S.W. 2d 636 [Tex. 1974])

In general, then, the exclusion of students from
school or from the extracurricula activities of the
school requires that the students in question present
a substantial or material danger to the school; otherwise, the courts may well rule against the disciplinary measures imposed by school authorities should the
case be litigated.

117

Discipline, Differential Treatment and Moral Development

Bassiouni's (1978) observation that the most important virtue of social institutions is justice was cited in a preceding chapter. Since the school is a social institution, and since youth tend to think in more nearly black and white terms than do most of their elders, it is particularly important to the youthful observer that the school reflect what he feels to be the ideal of justice. If a student perceives that the school is not just in its disciplinary procedures, he is likely to become hostile towards school authorities and he may become convinced that what he, himself, does, matters little since school discipline is arbitrary and capricious. These attitudes are obviously highly relevant to the primary goals of the school since the student who dislikes his teachers, for example, may prefer to fail academically rather than satisfy his teachers by passing. An educator who is disliked by students will have great difficulty in providing positive reinforcement, particularly social rewards, such as smiles, compliments, and the like, since the provision of such reinforcers implies that the provider is happy, or satisfied, with a student's performance; if the student dislikes an educator, probably doesn't want that educator to be happy or satisfied. Additionally, if the student perceives that discipline is administered without much regard for justice, his attitude that what he does doesn't matter because disciplinary measures are the result of luck or of the whims of powerful others may also be expected to affect his academic performance.

There is some research (Coleman, et. al., 1966; Gagne & Parshall, 1975; Lefcourt, 1972) which indicates that students who believe that what happens to them is the result of luck or of powerful others (external locus of control) do significantly less well in school than do students who believe what happens to them is the result of their own efforts (internal locus of control). The practice of raising or lowering a student's academic grades on the basis of his behavior in school is one example of a school policy which could result in the student's seeing the school as unjust and in his seeing his own efforts as irrelevant to what happens to him. The student may reason, "I know I'm better in math than anybody else in this class, but the teacher gives me the lowest grades because he doesn't like me." The teacher may reason,

"Jim is better than anybody else in the class in math, but, because of his acting-out, he makes it difficult for me to teach the other students. Anyway, even though Jim is doing better than the others in math, he could be doing twice as well if he would only try and stop misbehaving. I fail him so that he will straighten-up and get to work." Obviously, the student and the teacher are almost hopelessly divided in the preceding example. Justice dictates that the student who does well in math should receive a high grade in math. If that student's behavior is undesirable, a low grade should be given for school behavior, or deportment.

Students who believe that what happens to them is the result of luck or of the actions of powerful others (external locus of control), are more likely to be depressed (Blaney, 1977; Brannigan, Rosenberg, & Loprete, 1977; Evans & Wanty, 1979) and passive (Albert & Geller, 1978) than are those who believe that what happens to them is the result of their own actions or efforts (internal locus of control). The development of "I-ness", or a sense of self, may in part depend on a youngster's perception that authority figures react to her on the basis of her own actions rather than on the basis of authority figures' mood or whim (Donnewerth, et al, 1973). Depression often results when persons feel that they are helpless in affecting what they perceive to be necessary changes in their lives; therefore, youths who feel that their own efforts do not matter are likely to feel depressed as a result of this feeling of helplessness. Socially maladjusted youth often appear to be depressed (Chawst, 1967), and many teenage pregnancies may be the result of attempts to overcome depression through intense interpersonal relationships (Toolan, 1962). Since teenage pregnancies are often viewed as a type of discipline problem by the school, particularly since this often leads to the young mother's dropping out of school, the avoidance of the feelings of helplessness which accompany depression seems poignantly pertinent. Certainly, youngsters who feel depressed and helpless can not be expected to perform at an optimal level in academic subject matter or in their social interactions. In consideration of the foregoing, it becomes obvious that an important problem facing the school is that of forgoing disciplinary policies which will make a student aware of the fact that it is the student's actions which will determine the treatment accorded her by school authorities.

119

Internal locus of control students, who believe
that what happens to them is the result of their own
actions, are more difficult to control than are external locus of control students (Cravens & Worchel,
1977), who believe that what happens to them is the
result of luck or of important others. Further, students with an internal locus of control are more likely to become depressed and maladjusted under conditions of great helplessness than would be the case
with students who believe that luck and powerful
others are in control of what happens to them (Pittman
& Pittman, 1979). Consequently, it is particularly
important to involve internal locus of control students, who are often high achievers, in disciplinary
decision making. Internal locus of control students
believe that they are in control of their own desti-
nies; disciplinarians who contradict these students'
basic assumptions by not including these students in
the determination and enforcement of disciplinary
procedures, for example, may alienate students who
could otherwise have a salutary effect on the school
climate.

Illusions of justice

In the administration of justice, it is unques-
tionably important that the educator deal fairly with
students, but it is probably equally important that
students perceive that they have been given a fair
shake. In a previous chapter justice and fairness
were discussed as philosophical issues with sociological implications. In the present chapter the relationship of procedural justice to school discipline
has been examined, particularly as this applies to the
procedures which educators must follow in disciplining
students. We shall now turn our attention to justice
as a psychological issue which has sociological appli-
cations.

From a psychological stand point, the concept of
justice has been examined primarily from the point of
view of fairness in social exchange, or equity theory.
Equity is achieved when individual social participants
are similarly provided compensation which reflects
their relative contributions, i.e., greater compensation for greater contributions. Most kindergarten
children seem to understand and practice the principles of justice outlined by equity theory, though
girls seem to prefer the justice of parity (Leventhal
& Anderson, 1970). The justice of parity involves an

120

equal distribution of rewards, or compensation, regardless of each participant's relative contribution and personal interest in the division of those rewards. Obviously, it may not be necessary for the school to teach youngsters the principles of fairness outlined above. However, the more sophisticated concept of justice which considers the best interests of all parties based on the type of self-actualization of which each is capable, as discussed in an earlier chapter, might well need to be taught – not only to students but to educators, as well. Further, educators may expect sexual, and perhaps cultural, differences in youngsters' views of what is just, or fair. When determining school disciplinary policies, it might be wise for educators to engage in a candid give and take with students in order to determine which social transactions they see as fair or preferable. In awarding social recognition to students, as at school assemblies, for example, it would be important that students be in agreement with the principles of justice which the school is employing; otherwise, such awards and presentations would create more resentment than satisfaction.

There are indications (Folger, 1977) that youngsters' perceptions of what is just may be based on their recent experiences in improving their lot by means of their own actions. Youngsters whose fortunes are improved through their own efforts seem to develop higher expectations and greater dissatisfaction, regardless of the actual outcome, than is the case with students who have no voice in effecting imrovements in their lot (Folger, 1977). Consequently, the school which allows students greater voice in disciplinary matters may well have a student body which is seemingly less content than may be the case in an authoritarian school. However, seeming contentment and student apathy often coexist. An apathetic student body can not be expected to do as well academically as a student body which is actively involved in determining its own fate. Further, since the school is supposed to prepare students for later life, teaching students to take control of their own fate appears to be a highly desirable educational goal.

Educators who are involved in the administration of justice in school disciplinary procedures should be aware of the fact that their perceptions of a student's merits, or demerits, may be influenced by factors which are quite irrelevant to the problems under consideration. There are some indications that evaluators may perceive the persons they evaluate as significantly more emotionally mature and as having a greater sense of personal responsibility when the person being evaluated has social attitudes and opinions which are like those held by the evaluator (Good & Good, 1977). Though the previously mentioned study was not aimed at a school population, application of the findings to such a setting would lead one to believe that educators who work in multi-cultural environments may therefore expect to experience difficulty in properly evaluating students who differ from themselves; further, even when students are culturally similar, students' attitudes and opinions which are irrelevant to the disciplinary problem under consideration may be expected to influence the disciplinarian's judgement.

The traditional in loco parentis stance of the school often leads educators to adopt a paternalistic attitude towards students, an insidious type of "father knows best" attitude which robs students of the opportunity to be persons in their own right. A paternalistic attitude can be expected to result in unhappiness for those whose decisions are preempted; additionally, paternalism can be expected to result in general immaturity and stunted intelletual growth on the part of those who are not allowed to take an active role in their own lives. The rights of students seem to include the right to make mistakes on occasion (Matter of Panarella v. Birenbaum, 37 A. D. 2d 987) since this is an important part of the educational process.

Power and punishment

Educators should be prepared for student complaints of unfairness in regard to school rules, and students should be prepared to face these problems as another fact of life. Students are generally more concerned with the unfairness of enforcement of school rules than with the unfairness of the rules, themselves, and rightfully so. The injustices of history seem readily apparent in retrospect, but individuals tend to be blind to the injustices of their own times:

> Till 1487, anyone who knew how to read
> might commit murder as often as he pleased,
> with no other result than that of being

122

delivered to the ordinary [ecclesiastical authority] to make his purgation .... That this should have been the law for several centuries seems hardly credible, but there is no doubt that it was. Even after 1487 a man who could read could commit murder once with no other punishment than that of having M branded on the brawn of his left thumb.

(Stephen, 1883, pp. 463-464, according to Black, 1976, p. 66)

The preceding example of the laws of England prior to the sixteenth century seems shocking today, but it obviously was not anymore shocking in its time than was slavery in the eighteenth and nineteenth centuries. The affluent and powerful are more likely to complain to the police about the crimes of the poor than the reverse, and crimes by those of lower social status against those of higher social status are seen as more serious (Black, 1976). As will be seen, power and punishment are inversely related in the schools, as well.

Students, almost by definition, have a status which is subordinate to that of the teacher and the administrator. Therefore, offenses committed by students against the educator are generally seen as more serious than similar acts which are committed by the educator against the student. For example, many educators employ mild physical force, such as holding a student by the arm and "leading" him into or out of the classroom; if a student were to "lead" a teacher in this manner, it would be cause for disciplinary action. Students who have rigid "right" or "wrong" thinking patterns may have difficulty in dealing with what they may perceive as a double standard. Obviously, there are some important reasons for teachers' rights and privileges, but students are not usually taught these reasons, including the physical safety of the class, the socio-emotional comfort which is necessary to teaching and learning, etc.

Nevertheless, if students are fully respected as persons, as discussed in previous chapters, the discrepancy between the rights and privileges of the student and the educator should be minimized. There are some school amenities which serve to enhance the status of the educator while also distancing him from the students, such as a teacher's lounge into which no

123

students are allowed, or separate rest room facilities for faculty and students. Status enhancing provisions are important to social life, as indicated by the giving of awards at school assemblies, school honor rolls, etc. However, since the general poverty of most schools makes it difficult to provide status enhancing awards, those that do exist should be used to the greatest extent possible. Many youngsters could benefit from occasional visits to the teacher's lounge, such visits could be used either as status enhancing awards or as facilitators of communication and rapport between students and teachers. Similarly, the principal who takes a personal interest in student work on her visits to the classroom, or to whom students are sent for compliments on their work, can function as a status enhancer. Too often, principals and other administrators only see students when there is a problem; this may lead to negative conditioning towards administrators on the part of some students. Students who see administrators as a source of punishment, rather than of reward, will probably be reluctant to follow "their rules."

More powerful individuals are less likely to be punished for their offenses than are less powerful individuals, as any cursory comparison of the prison sentences for white collar crimes versus street crimes makes obvious. Student power is reflected by numerous variables, physical appearance, social class of the parents, etc. Very articulate students may be able to make their devious deeds palatable to school disciplinarians, while students of lesser verbal ability may be punished for the same misdeeds. Intelligent students are less likely to get caught than are students who are not intelligent. Also, adults are more likely to identify with the intelligent student, and, as a consequence, they are more likely to empathize with such students. A parent who is a physician is more likely to be able to effectively negotiate compassionate settlements between school authorities and an errant son than would be the case if the parent were a factory worker. It is important that school personnel be aware of the differential treatment which results from these power imbued personal characteristics. Obviously, it would seem desirable to minimize differential treatment which is simply the result of a student's power status if other students are to avoid feelings of anger and resentment against school authorities for what they may well perceive to be hypocrisy in the application of school rules.

Emotionally/morally gifted persons

As in the case of the greater society, the schools do not generally recognize those who are emotionally or morally gifted. Morality is understandably viewed as complex, but this complexity does not prevent society from judging those it perceives to be morally deficient; however, those who have reached advanced stages of moral development are hardly ever acknowledged, except after death, and, even then, only rarely. Similarly, the only levels of emotional adjustment which are differentiated from one another are those at the level of disturbance and at the level of "normalcy." Many schools presently have programs for almost every type of gifted student, including the psychomotor gifted, intellectually gifted, artistically gifted, etc., but the areas of morality and emotional sensitivity, or adjustment, are ignored. One reason for this, perhaps, is the emotionally loaded term "gifted." If the same logic were applied to the verbal designation used for the mentally retarded as is used for the gifted, the mentally retarded would be labeled "the cheated." Perhaps the implication of an endowment from God, or some supernatural force, which lurks behind the term gifted is subconsciously seen as being incompatible with emotional and moral development, which are viewed as being earned or worked towards. Though the mentally retarded are, in fact, often punished for their condition, hardly anyone would see such punishment as just, if it were properly understood. However, nearly everyone sees punishment for immoral behavior as just, and such behavior does, of course, often result from emotional maladjustment, so that the individual is in effect being punished for maladjustment, and this is generally viewed as just.

It may be more difficult, then, to acknowledge those who are morally or emotionally gifted since this indicates that they have earned their "giftedness," rather than having received it as an endowment, and, further, the implication is that they have outperformed those who must now pay tribute to them because they have worked harder than those who are not gifted thusly. In reality, of course, there may well be the same types of genetic predispositions of emotional adjustment as exist in other areas of human development, but such considerations would throw our judicial and penal systems into a state of shock, and the resulting immobility would create severe social problems until these considerations were incorporated into a different approach, if that is even possible. Consequently, it would appear desirable to use the term "advanced" rather than "gifted" when referring to individuals who are atypical in their development because of superior performance in some area of human development.

The increasing technological complexity of our world has brought with it an increase in the moral complexity of the decisions which must be made, examples of this include the possibility of saving the life of a severly deformed infant who will never be able to function in anything other than an institution, and who would have died of natural causes prior to recent medical advances, the decision to use, or not use, neutron bombs, which result in excruciating death while sparing property from destruction, the decision to spend money on national defense or on social programs, etc. At present, those who make decisions at the highest levels of government, those who, in effect, shape the social structure, have no training for their positions; hardly any other responsible positions in our society accommodate untrained personnel. It is not unusual for a national secretary of defense to be a trained physicist, or attorney, though the forementioned fields have no real relevance to decisions regarding national defense. Those at the highest levels of government are actually making moral decisions regarding the quality and duration of the lives of many millions of people, but they have had absolutely no formal training in morality, or in the development of sensitivity to the needs of others, because our schools do not provide such training, but what areas of human development could possibly be more important than those of morality and emotional sensitivity?

Reasons which are frequently advanced for avoiding instruction in morality include the separation of church and state and parental resistance to such instruction in the schools. However, the area of ethics is one which is considerably less controversial than that of morality, but schools do not teach courses in ethics, with the possible exception of a few college level courses in programs such as philosophy, medicine, or law. The area of development in emotional sensitivity is one which appears to not be seriously considered by hardly anyone, though in a world which is as culturally diverse as ours, it is difficult to understand how one might deal intelligently with those

126

who hold different ethical, or moral, convictions except through the application of emotional sensitivity to social problem solving.

Obviously, there are no black and white rules in ethics, morality, or emotional sensivity, nor can there be rigid curricula for instruction in these areas. As in the arts, where there are also no hard and fast rules, instruction in the area of ethics, morality, and emotional sensitivity would be given by those who are advanced, or gifted, in these areas. Though the adult world seems to revolve on committe work, little formal training in committee work is given in the schools. Instruction in ethics, morality, and emotional sensitivity would seem to lend itself well to committee work, where peer instruction could assure that the material remains relevant and within the grasp of the students involved. Reading the observations of the acknowledged moral leaders of history, such as those of Christ, Gandhi, or Martin Luther King, would certainly be an appropriate part of such curricula. It seems ironic that the history books and social studies books of the schools pay considerably more attention to the words and deeds of men of war than to those of men and women of peace. It is also unfortunate that the lives of men and women who lead lives of love and peace, but who fail to become famous, are ignored in the curricula of the schools. Students should be helped to understand the greatness of those who quietly weave patterns of love and peace in the lives of others, regardless of the fame which these individulas may or may not achieve; otherwise, students are led to believe that the important thing is to make a grand splash, and the easiest way to do this is often by creating serious disciplinary problems in the school!

Those whose primary professional responsibilities include the administration of student discipline should ideally be individuals who are morally and emotionally advanced, or gifted, and who have had formal training in the areas of ethics, morality, and emotional sensitivity to the needs of others. Such individuals would then be able to instruct students in these vital areas, in addition to punishing students for their infractions. It would seem important to begin this instructional approach to disciplinary problems as soon as possible in a child's school career. Though teachers must be expected to handle most disciplinary problems themselves, they are cer-

127

tainly entitled to the services of a specialist in this extremely complex area, and meeting the qualifications for school administration does not better prepare one to deal with disciplinary problems than does qualifying for a teaching position.

References

Albert M., & Geller, E. Perceiving control as a mediator of learned helplessness. *American Journal of Psychology*, 1978, 91, 389-400.

Bassiouni, M. C. *Substantive Criminal Law*. Springfield, IL: Charles C. Thomas, 1978.

Black, D. *The Behavior of Law*. New york: Academic Press, 1976.

Blackstone, W. *Commentaries on the Laws of England*. Oxford: Clarendon Press, 1976.

Bolmeier, E. C. *Legality of Student Disciplinary Practices*. Charlottesville, VA: The Michie Company, 1976.

Blaney, P. H. Contemporary theories of depression: Critique and comparison. *Journal of Abnormal Psychology*, 1977, 86, 203-223.

Bowdoin, W. R. Balancing *in loco parentis* and the Constitution: Defining the limits of authority over Florida's public high school students. *University of Florida Law Review*, 1974, 26, 271-288.

Brannigan, G. C., Rosenberg, L. A., & Loprete, I. J. Internal-external explectancey, maladjustment and psychotherapeutic intervention. *Journal of Personality Assessment*, 1977, 41, 71-78.

Chawst, J. Depressive reactions manifested among adolescent delinquents. *American Journal of Psychotherapy*, 1967, 21, 575-584.

Children's Defense Fund. Report of the Children's Defense Fund of the Washington Research Project, Inc., "Children Out of School in America," 1974.

Cravens, R. W., & Worchel, P. The differential effects of rewarding and coercive leaders on group members differing in locus of control. *Journal of Personality*, 1977, 45, 150-168.

References

Coleman, J. S., Campbell, E. Q., Hobson, C. J., McPartland, J., Mood, A. M., Weinfeld, F. D., & York, R. L. Equality of educational opportunity. Washington, D. C.: United States Government Printing Office, 1966.

Connors, E. T. Student Discipline and the Law. Bloomington, IN: Phi Delta Kappa Educational Foundation, 1979.

Donnewerth, G., Teichman, M., & Foa, U. Cognitive differentiation of self and parents in delinquent and non-delinquent girls. British Journal of Social and Clinical Psychology, 1973, 12, 144-152.

Evans, R. G., & Wanty, D. W. I-E Scale responses as a function of subject mood level. Journal of Personality Assessment. 1979, 43, 166-170.

Folger, R. Distributive and procedural justice: Combined impact of "voice" and improvement on experienced inequity. Journal of Personality and Social Psychology, 1977, 35, 108-119.

Gagne, E. E., & Parshall, H. The effects of locus of control and goal setting on persistance at a learning task. Child Study Journal, 1975, 5 193-199.

Good, L. R. & GOod, K. C. Influence of attitude similarity on parole recommendations. The Journal of Social Psychology, 1977, 101, 135-137.

Lefcourt, H. M. Recent developments in the study of locus of control. In B. A. Maher (Ed.), Progress in Experimental Personality Research. Vol. 6. New York: Academic Press, 1972.

Leventhal, G., & Anderson, D. Self-interest and the maintenance of equity. Journal of Personality and Social Psychology, 1970, 15, 312-316.

Pittman, N. L., & Pittman, T. S. Effects of amount of helplessness training and I-E locus of control on mood and performance. Journal of Personality and Social Psychology, 1979, 37, 39-47.

References

Platt, A. M. The Child Savers: The Invention of Delinquency. Chicago: University of Chicago Press, 1977.

Schimmel, D., & Fischer, L. The Civil Rights of Students. New York: Harper & Row, 1975.

Stephen, J. F. A History of the Criminal Law of England. Vol. 1. London: MacMillan, 1883.

Toolan, J. Depression in children and adolescents. American Journal of Orthopsychiatry, 1962, 32, 404-415.

Chapter Seven

School Discipline: A Retrospective and Prospective View

In this chapter an attempt will be made at tracing trends in the development of school behavior and school discipline in the United States. Obviously, the rather bold generalizations which are required for the foregoing purpose will admit of many exceptions, but the attempt of this chapter is the prediction of future trends. It is only through an understanding of the present and future directions of school behavior and school discipline that educators may tune and adjust development in their schools so that they are able to take advantage of prevailing winds while holding to the charted course of their choosing. The trends in school discipline would seem to indicate the following: 1. an ever increasing emphasis on individual rights and recognition of the child as a person; 2. a concomitant emphasis on verbalizations of social expectations with fewer nonverbalized, or core, expectations; 3. a broadening of the boundaries of acceptable behavior; 4. a decrease in the use of physical force and punishment. Prior to discussing the implications of these trends for the future, we shall very briefly examine the status of children historically.

Status of Children and the Schools

The status of children from biblical times through much of the twentieth century was that of a possession of their fathers. Consequently, rules of conduct were largely dependent on the convenience of adults, and particularly of fathers; discipline was often harsh because the comfort of adults was the primary concern of disciplinarians. An example of the disciplinary procedures which were available includes the following:

If any child [ren] above sixteen years old and of sufficient understanding shall curse or smite their natural father or mother, they shall be put to death, unless it can be sufficiently testified that the parents have been very unchristianly negligent in the education of such children, or so provoked them by extreme and cruel correction that they have been forced thereunto

to preserve themselves from death or maiming
...

(Mass. Records, III [1854], 101, according
to Bremner, 1970)

Prior to the twentieth century, and for some years
thereafter, children were often financial assets to
their farming families since much of the farm work
could be performed by children; further, the lack of
child labor laws often caused children to become
financial assets in the cities, as well. In a time
when retirement plans were unknown, children became a
type of social security for their parents. Religious
convictions also stressed the importance of children,
and of the care of children, for the salvation of
mankind. Children were not to be "spoiled" under any
circumstances. In colonial days the churches generally provided a basic education for those children who
had the ability, deportment, and intelligence to
attend. The teachers who were hired by the churches
were expected to be models of virtue for their students, and students and teachers alike were expected
to confrom to very strict rules of conduct.

Darwin's theories, published in the mid-
nineteenth century, and those of the eugenists, led to
the application of biological principles to human
society, or Social Darwinism. Social Darwinism led to
a belief that all was right with the world, i.e., the
rich and successful were "fit" and the poor and ignorant were "unfit," their very existence being a threat
to the gene pool. Obviously, this type of thinking
meant that the schools were primarily for a social and
intellectual elite. Spenser (1896) believed that
children should learn that life consists of a grim
struggle for existence in which one should aspire to
goals which are appropriate to one's place in society.

The doctrine of "Manifest Destiny" reflected the
belief that English should become the language of the
world, Christianity its religion, and Anglos its
rulers. The "melting pot" society was one in which
persons from inferior cultures were to adopt Anglo
characteristics and conform to the superior Anglo
value system. The schools were not tolerant of behaviors which deviated from the established Anglo norms.
Educators, whose formal training did not equip them to
handle anything other than the teaching of standard

regimen to typical Anglo children, seem to have adopted a supercilious attitude towards immigrants, whose
adjustment to U.S. society seems to have been assumed
by privately sponsored settlement houses (Higham,
1971). Similarly, although the courts, under the old
English law of "parens patriae", assumed responsibility for children whose families could not, or did not,
care for them, the government did not provide services
for such children. The lack of provisions for dependent persons is well illustrated by the case of an
eighteen year old girl, whose family was imprisoned,
"... and thus left without a home, she was forced to
make her lodging in a brothel on the outskirts of the
city. Next morning she applied to the judge to be re-
committed to prison "for protection" against specified
carnal outrages required of her and submitted to ..."
(Dugdale, 1877, p. 8). Indeed, Spenser (1864), a
leading writer of the time, believed that natural laws
cause intelligence to be as important as physical fit-
ness and, he reasoned, just as those with severe physical problems die of natural causes, those with intellectual or moral deficiences should be allowed to die
as a natural result of their failings and limitations
since society could not be expected to improve if such
individuals were allowed to taint the genetic pool.
Obviously, the foregoing philosophy spoke against
special provisions for children with learning or behavior problems, who were simply excluded from school,
thus eliminating many possible behavior problems.
Some leading psychologists, such as Edward Thorndike
(1913), also saw intelligence as primarily hereditary
and advocated limited vocational education for those
with learning or behavior problems.

With the advent of the twentieth century, some
educators, such as Dewey, suggested that schools
should supplement the family as socializing agents and
abandon elitist attitudes towards education which were
prevalent in prior centuries. Dewey believed that the
schools should cause children to become " 'saturated'
with the spirit of service" (Hofstader, 1963, p. 379).
Although many large cities did provide special schools
for truants and incorrigibles in the late nineteenth
and early twentieth century (Seaver, 1894), school
discipline does not appear to have been a major social
issue, as recent Gallup polls indicate is the case at
present. However, the passage of compulsory school
attendance laws did increase the disciplinary burden
of the school.

Increasing industrialization and the passage of child labor laws decreased the possibilities of gainful employment for children and youth. Widespread industrialization also created a need for experts of various sorts. The many broken homes and destitute children who emerged from the Depression of the 1930's made it clear to governmental agencies that children were in need of the services of experts if those functions which were formerly the sole responsibility of the family were to be provided at all. However, expert services were usually available only in the cities and, in the 1920's and 1930's, rural children were seen as being significantly more poorly adjusted than were children living in the cities (White House Conference on Child health and Protection, 1930, according to Beck, 1973). Further, the responsibilities for the social welfare of children began to shift from private charities to public agencies, including the schools.

As might be expected, given the wide latitude allowed the schools in punishing and expelling students in the nineteenth century, there was relatively little violent crime in the schools. However, Doyle (1978), notes that in so far as the problems of day to day classroom discipline were concerned, the tasks of managing a classroom in the 1890's were very similar, if somewhat more complex, than is the case today. Feldhusen (1978) also notes that 19th century schooling was aimed at training the child in moral discipline through the use of punishment, particularly of floggings, but pupil expectations of punishment may have lessened their sensitivity to it as it might be viewed today. The isolated teacher of the nineteenth century, who had access to no support services except for a few schools for truant children, obviously could not be expected to cope with classroom discipline problems in the way in which these problems are dealt with today.

Discipline Today and Yesterday

Kaestle (1978) notes that classrooms of the nineteenth century frequently held thirty to eighty students and therefore often required silence and regimentation; as might be expected, given the severity of school discipline, parents and the schools were often at odds with one another, school reports were often filled with anti-parental propaganda and parents were frequently accused of undermining school disciplinary procedures:

> As schools became more graded and students more classified, the informal, chaotic, individualized instructional world of eighteenth century classrooms gave way to a well-defined lock-step curriculum. Schools thus became in some regards like factories, but not necessarily because they were mimicking factories, or preparing children to work in factories. Rather, both the workplace and the schools as well as other nineteenth-century institutions, were partaking of the same ethos of efficiency, manipulation, and mastery.

(Kaestle, 1978, p. 7)

The twentieth century saw the coming of experts in education, psychology, and social work who were able to open up the lines of communication between the home and the school, while also applying specialized, and more sophisticated, methods of social control and instruction. Though there was considerable opposition to the use of behavior modification in the mid-nineteenth century because many parents and professionals saw the use of this approach as infringing on an individual's free will, and as being morally repugnant, the frequent use of behavior modification in eclectic approaches led to its gradual acceptance as the reinforcers used in behavior modification came to be compared to the natural reinforcers of everyday life and to man-made reinforcers, such as pay checks, with the result that the presumed coerciveness of the approach came to be overlooked , or considered to be nonexistent. The scientific nature of the behavior modification approach to behavioral control, e.g., it is quantifiable, permits of rigorous hypothesis testing and evaluation of results, and is replicable, lent increased prestige and credibility to those who used such approaches, including educators. In recent years education has become increasingly more specialized and it has become increasingly difficult for parents to challenge the expertise of those who are in charge of educational programs. This sometimes misplaced reliance on the good intentions and competence of the experts in education and psychology encourages the passage of laws which enhance the power of the parents and the child in their relationship to the school, as with Public Law 94-142, which gives parents many

137

rights in deciding the placement and program which is to be provided their handicapped child.

The ever increasing emphasis on individual rights requires constant vigilance on the part of school authorities, whose dilemma it is to protect the rights of the majority while often protecting them from the deviant few, whose rights must also be protected. The current emphasis on the rights of the individual is a luxury which soon disappears in times of difficulty or stress, even in countries that pride themselves on the rights of the individual. When individual rights are stressed, it becomes necessay to verbalize those rights and to clearly define violations of expected norms. This need for verbalization will result in a smaller set of core expectations, or unwritten and unspoken laws. When laws are written and/or spoken, they are easier to challenge than is the case when laws are unwritten or unspoken. When laws are written and spoken, the logic and fairness of the law can be questioned, but when a norm, or expectation, is unwritten or unspoken, it is impossible to challenge it since it appears not to exist. For example, the social norms of most countries have long dictated that women should be held in an inferior state and it has been impossible for women to challenge this expectation since it is unwritten and has been unspoken until fairly recently. When a woman in the United States complains that she does not have her constitutional rights the response is often that she does have her rights in the many laws which have been passed, but which are not a part of the Constitution. There is no way that a woman can prove that she does not have her Constitutional rights since there is no written or spoken law, or expectation, that she does not have those rights; fighting for women's rights often resembles shadow boxing in that the objection can find no target - how can a woman insist that she has no equal rights when there is no law that states that she has no rights.

Consequently, the schools can be expected to experience increasing difficulties as more and more of the expectations held by the schools become written and spoken. Prior to rules regarding women's athletic teams, a woman, or girl, might protest against the lack of opportunities for women in sports, though such protest was in any case unlikely since there were no written or spoken expectations against opportunities for women in sports - it simply seemed that such opportunities were impossible for mysterious reasons which were known by no-one, but which were in any case obvious since there were no opportunities, and if there could have been opportunities there would have been opportunities; such circular reasoning is difficult to overcome, however illogical it may be. When rules and expectations are written and/or spoken, they become real problems rather than shadows and it is possible to mount logical protests against them. As logical protests are made, it becomes more and more difficult to defend rules and expectations and the boundries of acceptable behavior are expanded as the logic against them can not be refuted. Logical protests against unwritten and unspoken rules and expectations are difficult, or impossible, since such rules and expectations can not be analyzed, and logic requires analysis.

Since it is impossible to specify every conceivable situation which might arise and to which a given rule might apply, a decrease in core expectations, or in unverbalized rules, necessarily results in a decrease in rules and a broadening of the boundaries of acceptable behavior. Further, the expectation that rules should be verbalized rather than merely taken for granted results in an increase in the testing of the boundaries of acceptable behavior. Thus, students in the 1950's took it for granted that only certain types of clothes were acceptable for school, but students of the late 1960's rebelled against what they perceived to be the misuse of authority in regard to the Vietnam War and the treatment of minority groups - with the result that they also rebelled against the expectations of authority in regard to dress, drugs, and sex. This rebellion led to the verbalization of rules which had formerly been nonverbalized, or core, expectations, but the fact that core expectations had to be verbalized meant that they were no longer core expectations, they were expectations that could be challenged since they were clearly defined.

The fact that rules can be questioned, or challenged, also means that authority is placed in a defensive position. When authorities are placed on the defensive in justifying the rules, they are less likely to formulate rules and they are more likely to make the rules very specific. Consequently, the shrinking of unspoken rules, or core expectations, generally results in a greater number of spoken, or written, rules, but behavioral limitations are reduced when the rules are verbalized because less is left to the imagination and because those who verbalize the rules need to be fairly specific. Thus, there was a time when boys were expected to have "masculine", i.e., short, haircuts, but as boys came to prefer longer hair styles it became necessary for schools to verbally specify the acceptable length for a boy's hair, but specifying the length in inches was hopeless unless principals and teachers were to be expected to walk around with rulers in their hands while taking daily measurements of their students' hair; consequently, acceptable hair length was usually specified in terms of its relationship to the ear or to the collar, which was still considerably longer than had been customary prior to the time when verbalized rules for hair length had been required.

There has been a decrease in the use of physical force and punishment over the years as the rights of the child have become almost as well established as are the rights of an adult. The general distaste for force which has resulted, in part, at least, from the possibility of mass destruction on a global scale, has led educators and others to mothball their paddles. The complexities of a world of gray have made the quick and simplistic punishments of yesterday inappropriate. The fact that children have rights has resulted in serious difficulties where questions of guilt or innocence may exist because the state of having rights means that what may at first appear to be an offense, or deviant behavior, may actually be behavior which is within one's rights; further, the state of having rights means that some time and expense must be spent in determining the guilt or innocence of a student, which leads to fewer accusations and to fewer disciplinary actions as the authorities try to avoid substantial losses in time and energy. The fact that authorities attempt to ignore situations which might cost them unnecessary time and energy means that they allow the boundaries of acceptable behavior to expand further, and this further expansion of acceptable behavior means that more serious misbehaviors are likely to be ignored in the future.

Discipline Today and Tomorrow

Obviously there is a point of diminishing returns insofar as permissiveness and individual rights are concerned. As third world countries become better armed and more aggressive in their demands for an

140

equal share of the world's resources, it may be expected that the favored nations will become less favored and poorer. Poverty often makes some rights less likely. For example, if people are engrossed in activities which will provide them with food and shelter, they are less likely to be concerned about due process rights for students which will require an expenditure of human resources which might otherwise be used in fulfilling basic needs. Similarly, if there are many students who require a basic education, but few resources for the provision of such an education, students may well be required to perform in a militant fashion. Economic recessions and depressions are likely to result in a reduction of individual rights for students, but a concomitant reduction in supervision may act as a braking force in this trend. Thus, under conditions of poverty, students may find that they no longer have due process rights because the shortage of administrators makes it impossible for the schools to spend any time listening to students' complaints of foul play when they are suspended from school for something they claim they have not done. On the other hand, that same shortage of administrators may mean that fewer students will get caught doing things that they are not supposed to do. On the whole, however, it must be expected that students will have fewer rights as the schools are provided with less money.

At the present time world peace appears to be contingent a balance in the arms race between the Soviet Union and the United States; however, as small militant countries increase the destructive power of their bombs and other military equipment, it is to be expected that the demands of such countries will be seen as important in maintaining world peace. The demands of the less powerful nations for natural resources will require that wealthier nations provide scarce recources to those countries, but it is probable that wealthier nations will also attempt diplomatic negotiations in an attempt at making economic changes come at as slow a rate as possible - thus, the former insistence on rapid change as a way of obtaining wealth in the form of economic progress is likely to give way to an attempt at making changes as slowly as possible so that present resources are retained. An attempt at maintaining the status quo is likely to be felt in the schools as well- where the expectation that students' rights will continue to expand and proliferate is likely to give way to an attempt at hold-

141

ing on to rights which are eroding away. Students are generally an impoverished and dependent group of individuals who are among the first to lose privileges when the going gets rough. At the present time of federal cut backs in allocations to the states for education, there is considerable thought being given to an elimination, or a redefinition, of the P.L. 94-142 law which deals with the rights of handicapped children. Times of economic recession and depression frequently herald an increase in property crimes as the destitute attempt to get their basic needs filled in whatever way then can, and large cities in the United States which have high rates of unemployment frequently have crime waves in the public schools. An increase in crime within the school is also likely to result in a loss of individual rights as the school enforces its version of marshall law in an attempt at saving life and limb.

Consequently, the advances of the recent past in the area of students' rights are not likely to be maintained in the future given the economic forecasts for this country. Tight money, tight purse strings and shrinking purses are likely to result in greater difficulties in the area of social mobility. Youngsters from the lower social classes are less likely to find the doors of opportunity open to them in the form of college scholarships and loans, they are also less likely to be able to find employment. Schools which educate such children are likely to become more rigid in their disciplinary policies and less positive, and more negative, in terms of the school climates which they establish. Black (1976) has observed that the law does not treat everyone equally and that the less powerful individuals in a society are those who are under the contol of the law, which, after all, has been written by those who are more powerful. Blue collar crime is always treated more seriously than is white collar crime. Stealing a car frequently carries a heavier penalty than does tax fraud or embezzlement because those who steal cars generally come from the lower, less powerful, social classes; whereas, those who embezzle frequently come from the upper, more powerful, social classes. Similarly, the more permissive schools are frequently found in middle or upper class neighborhoods while more restrictive schools frequently characterize lower class neighborhoods. If our social class system should become a social caste system because of unemployment and lack of educational opportunities, it is likely that the school climates

142

of schools in poorer neighborhoods will deteriorate and that school policies will become more and more restrictive and oppressive as both educators and students perceive that the school's function is one of maintaining students in holding pattern until graduation and probable under-employment or unemployment.

It would appear, then, that student rights are more tightly tied to economic conditions than to a gradual evolution of law in the realm of human rights. The maintenance of human rights, and a defense of those rights, frequently requires an expenditure of human resources which can not be afforded when the economy is poor. Although students are unlikely to lose many of the rights they have won over past decades, the enforcement of those rights is likely to be reduced. Since school discipline is closely tied to the rights which are granted students, any change in students' rights, or in the enforcement of those rights, may be expected to affect school discipline.

Not only is proverty likely to reduce the enforcement of individual rights, but it is also likely to reduce the recognition of the child as a person. Recognition of the person requires an acknowledgement of the unique characteristics of the person and a recognition of the unique pattern of development which characterizes individual human beings. Schools which operate on tight budgets must treat students as groups rather than as individuals. Further, schools which operate in areas of poverty are not likely to encourage unique patterns of development among students since such students often can be expected to share in a common fate, such as unemployment, which makes their patterns of development seemly less interesting and important than might be the case if the school perceives itself as preparing students for Ivy League Colleges. Schools which take little interest in the students as individuals are likely to have fairly strict and rigid disciplinary policies since every student is seen as being like every other student and treating students autocratically makes sense when they are all seen as having been cut from the same pattern and going into the same box. Schools which can not afford to individualize their programs are also likely to experience greater difficulty in experiencing satisfaction as a result of their educational efforts; such schools are likely to have a fairly high rate of failure among their students and the blame and frustration which accompanies such failure may often

143

create hostility between the educator and the student. Frustration generally breeds aggression. Under these conditions, it is likely that discipline will become increasingly punitive and inflexible as educators are overwhelmed with disciplinary problems and simply attempt to keep afloat.

Yet another potential threat to the rights of students in future years lies in the ever increasing degree of specialization to which they are exposed. Increasingly, students are dealt with by specialists who may adopt a medical model approach to deviant behavior. In the medical model those who are different, or deviants, are seen as being "sick" and in need of "normalization". Important subtle differences exist in seeing one who is different as being sick and in need of treatment versus being bad and in need of punishment. The attribution of sickness implies that the person has not chosen, nor would he chose, his present state if he were able to do otherwise. It also usually implies that the sick person can be made well by those who are wiser, stronger, or more skilled, than he. On the other hand, a person who is regarded as "bad" is often regarded as one who has his reasons and as one who has made his choice. The "bad" person may be punished by those who are more virtuous, but the very fact that this person has willfully chosen to be bad is accepted as proof that virtue does not appeal to him. If many rational persons choose to be "bad", one would eventually want to examine one's assumptions about what is "good", while examining further the attraction of that which is "bad". However, if many helpless persons are "sick", the only question which needs to be asked is "how do we stop the epidemic". Social change would be exceedingly difficult in a therapeutic state. The criminal can make a social statement, he can take a stand; the patient can only attempt to resist treatment.

The medical model also includes the assumption that therapeutic services may be rendered only by specialists. Thus, the teacher does not act as a counselor, the counselor does not engage in psychotherapy, and the psychologist does not teach - each specialist performs only a very restricted set of services. In this way, the attitudes of non-professionals nad professionals towards the youngster take on a type of technicians' mentality. The youngster is seen as one who will be "fixed" at the appropriate garage - if a stop at the psychiatrist's office doesn't cure him, a good dose of education may. If the student happens to be in need of one person who cares about his mental health while also caring about his physical health and his education, if the youngster needs someone who in some sense loves him, he is not likely to find this person in his weekly list of appointments.

A more appropriate focus for school discipline would be an inter-disciplinary model. The interdisciplinary model would attempt to de-specialize services to youth while minimizing stigma. At the core of such a model would be the development of a horizontal relationship, rather than a vertical relationship, between the adult and the youth. The emphasis of such a model would be prevention rather than cure. A problem which has not yet wholly surfaced cannot be neatly labeled and packaged for treatment by a specialist. Prevention necessitates an inter-disciplinary model. Professionals who adopt and inter-disciplinary aproach will find it possible to focus directly on the needs of a particular youngster - rather than finding it necessary to give fragmented and depersonalized services.

Although the relatively new concept of child advocacy fits the multi-disciplinary model nicely, definitions of "child advocacy" by various federal commissions have depicted the child advocate as one who is a liaison between the community agencies and clients (Joint Commission on Mental Health of Children, 1969; White House Conference on Children, Forum 25, 1970) - from the technicians' viewpoint, one who refers a youngster and his family to the right fix-it shop. A warm human relationship with a significant other over an extended period of time does not seem to be an integral part of the federal commissions' child advocacy model at the present time - the idea of the child advocate as a professional who is skilled in a variety of disciplines, and one who invites close, horizontal, relationships with youngsters, seems highly desirable.

Futuristic Discipline and Prevention

If serious discipline problems are to be avoided in the schools, it is necessary that students be as well adjusted as possible. Adequate adjustment may necessitate the fulfillment of certain basic needs in

145

a given period of a child's life. The occurrence of critical periods has been well established by ethologists. Conrad Lorenz (1937) identified a critical period for some species of birds during which "imprinting" takes place. During this critical period, usually during the first few hours after hatching, birds tend to follow the first moving object they see, as they would normally follow their mother; if the moving object is a bird of a different species, the bird imprinted will later attempt to mate only with the adopted species. The term "critical period" implies that a given behavior must be acquired within a particular time if it it to be expressed normally. Many investigators prefer the term "sensitivity period", which implies that certain behaviors are more easily and efficiently acquired during the time when the skill or behavior is just emerging, which is usually also the period of fastest growth for that skill. Fortunately, it would not be ethical to experiment in order to determine whether human beings have critical periods, but it seems well established that they do have sensitivity periods, particularly in the areas of language development and sexual identity. The period during which a behavior makes its first appearance seems to be the time when the establishment of that behavior is most precarious (Scott & Marston, 1950, according to Robinson & Robinson, 1976). Failure to pass a critical period results in impairment of subsequent development and may lead to a cumulative deficit. Again, ethology provides us with examples of various species of birds which know parts of the species song when quite young. However, there is a short "pre-pubertal" period during which a bird must be exposed to the entire song of the species in order to learn it properly - if it is heard before or after this period, it will not be learned. Not learning the species song at the appropriate time will lead to cumulative deficits since the species song is needed for territorial defense and for mating opportunities to occur.

The critical period concept implies the existence of stages of development - postulated by Erikson (1963) for human psycho-social development and by Piaget (1969) for intellectual development. Limitations in experimentation with human beings makes definitive statements about the existence of critical periods among humans impossible. Nevertheless, the very frequent failure of rehabilitative efforts and the tragic expense of human life and property demand that prevention rather than "cure" be the focus of disciplinary activity. A surrogate mother or father might help the seven year old child whose parents are abusive or disinterested, but such a surrogate may not be of any use for the same child at age fourteen when many of his problems may be beyond amelioration. If there are human critical periods, as seems to be the case at present, society must take great care to provide children with their developmental requirements at the appropriate time.

Although a knowledge of many disciplines can enrich the relationship which an adult develops with a child or an adolescent, a relationship seems crucial if the youth is to be helped in developing towards adulthood. As will be seen, this meaningful adult could be any one of many professionals or non-professionals, and it is doubtful that such persons could be "assigned" a youngster with very much effectiveness - except when they are performing their more traditional roles. The caring relationship which must be established is based on innumerable personality variables - making effective case assignments difficult, if not utterly impossible. Consequently, the multi-disciplinary approach must be an attitude. The "professional" fear of getting "too involved" with a youngster must be abandoned. Professionals should desire personal involvement with a youngster and they should be ready to support long term commitments to such youngsters when they encounter juveniles with whom a relationship seems possible and desirable. Program administrators should include records of this type of involvement in their evaluations of professional work. Youngsters should be viewed as consumers who can evaluate the providers of services they have received - especially over long periods of time and in the course of follow-up studies which take place after program completion.

Prevention and Client Prestige

The prestige of the client very often determines the social structure of the agency which deals with his problem. One who is an adult has more prestige than one who is "just a child". Further, one who works with adults, directly or indirectly, tends to have more prestige than one who works with children, the corporate president has more prestige than the superintendent of schools, the high school teacher has more prestige than the kindergarten teacher. Perhaps, then, it should surprise no-one that professionals often prefer to confer with professionals, or other adults, rather than with their child client. Making referrals and recommendations, or perceiving referrals and recommendations, and having conferences, are often times ways of avoiding direct contact with the child client.

The frustrations which are frequently encountered in working with children may also help to explain the professional inclination for working with other professionals rather than directly with the child. One need not accept responsibility for failure if several professionals are involved and no-one has helped the child. Further, the administration of a battery of tests in order to learn more about the child's abilities, disabilities, likes, and dislikes, seems considerably more professional, and, by implication, worthy of higher salaries, than simply asking the child directly.

People in the Unites States are under a constant barrage of advertising which is likely to increase in intensity in future years - with the result that reality will come to be more, and more, determined through advertising, e.g., new cars are desirable, one soap is better than another, attractive clothing is essential and designer jeans are to be preferred. The value and prestige of products and, by implication, of people, seems to be manipulated by the media to an extent which used to be possible only for the churches. It is assumed that advertisements which say, "Vote for Bill Franks" will help Bill get elected. Recent Gallup polls indicate that young Americans appear to be getting more materialistic in their values and ambitions and it may be that the public media contribute to this. Perhaps there is presently a need for "people values" to be given equal time in the public media. The fact that school budgets are among the first items to be cut in economically difficult times, with disastrous effects on school programs, school climate, and school discipline, may indicate that present values are inappropriate - and there is every reason to believe that things will not spontaneously improve. If social values are to improve, those who are most involved in passing on social values must help those values improve. One might envision, for example, happy people who are happy because they love and are loved presenting their side of the story to a television audience; such persons might admit to not being able to afford designer jeans and not caring about new cars while emphasizing the happines they find in loving others. In similar advertisements one might indicate that a person who has been poured into designer jeans and tucked into a new car might prefer having someone to love. The importance of children as people can only be understood in terms of love and respect for people. Adults are often respected because of their status in the community, because of their talents, because of their wealth, and so forth. Children, on the other hand, are mostly children - their value to the community can not usually be determined according to the products they can afford, the positions they hold, or the power they wield. Though it surprises no-one that the worth of children is not a focus of radio or TV advertising, it is very ironic that children do not learn about children in school. If children are important, and hardly anyone would deny that they are, why are they not included in history and social studies. Shouldn't children study about children from the early grades? Most of the children in our schools will never take courses in child development or family living. When such children come from very small nuclear families, as is frequently the case in times of declining births and increasing divorces, they are unlikely to understand the value of children as human beings who generate love and help to make life meaningful, but who, in turn, have particular needs which must often be met in particular ways. If educators want the general public and other professionals to see children, and working with children, as important, they should help educate children as to the importance of children by including children in the regular school curriculum. The inclusion of basic instruction in psychology and sociology, as well as actual supervised experience in working with children should be an extremely important part of the curriculum in schools for future years. School discipline is ultimately an attempt at inculcating particular values and standards of behavior. The more self-evident and attractive the school's values are, the less punitive the school discipline needs to be and the more likely it is that children will receive the help and attention they require.

Prevention: School Discipline for the Future

Mobility, social stress, and one parent families are all likely to increase in future years. As a result of these and other factors, it seems likely that

149

the school will be required to provide ever greater numbers of services to children whose home lives can not meet all of their needs. An acknowledgement of human critical periods, or sensitivity periods, places great responsibility on the school. If sensitivity periods in socio-emotional development do exist, as it seems they may, it is important to provide surrogate parents to children at the time when children typically need parental figures most if such persons are missing from a child's life, for example. The schools are presently very rigid in the roles they assign teachers. If the greatly varying needs of children are to be met at the time that these needs arise, teachers must be given greater flexibility in their job descriptions. Teachers would be ideal as child advocates whose primary function is to help children meet their basic needs. If children cannot be expected to learn school subjects until their basic needs are met, and if a teacher's job is to teach subject matter, then teachers also have the resopnsibility of helping children meet their basic needs. A hungry child cannot learn math, and educators should be instrumental in assuring that their students are not hungry. Similarly, an unhappy child who feels that he has no motherly love cannot be expected to behave in school or to learn social skills, and educators should make every attempt in helping to solve such problems. Teachers who function as child advocates could be seen as having varying work schedules and unpredictable duties which would depend on the particular needs of a specific child. Rather than punishing the first grader who acts up and refuses to do his work because he is constantly seeking teacher attention, the child advocate would provide the child with the attention he needs before school and after school, as well as in the classroom situation. The child advocate would be a roving trouble shooter for the school-such a person might help to identify problems, solve problems, provide services to children, teachers, and families, and follow-up on the solutions. It is difficult for teachers to meet deep needs for affection because children know that the teacher cares for them only while they are in a particular class - the teacher can not make long term commitments because he is hired to teach a class for a given period of time. The child advocate, on the other hand, might work with the same child, or children, for an extensive length of time, and such persons might be hired on the basis of their commitments to remaining in the community and being an active member of the community. Such a system would be preferable to the use of school social workers whose commitment is usually to the co-ordination of school and family interactions rather than to the para-educational needs of the child as an individual.

Obviously, the child advocate model for school discipline would not eliminate discipline problems. Healthy, happy children can, and do, present problems in discipline, but such children are likely to engage in acts of creative deviance rather than in acts of destructive deviance. A major theme of this book has been that deviant behavior, including school discipline problems, can be highly desirable. However, students who engage in anti-social behavior must often be punished in ways which cause pain to themselves and to their disciplinarians, as well. Further, poorly adjusted students often engage in deviant acts which are harmful to themselves and to others. It would seem, then, that the emphasis of discipline for the future should be adjustment of the student, with a view towards prevention of punishment, rather than the present emphasis on law and order.

Structure of Reference Group Expectations:
Past and Future

Past

deviance

Future

deviance

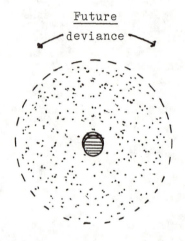

  core - expectations - unwritten,
unspoken rules

  written and spoken rules governing behavior

- - - - - - testable boundries of behavior
(applicable rules unclear)

region of deviance
(limitless possibilities)

References

Beck, R. White House Conferences on Children: An Historical Perspective. _Harvard Educational Review_, 1973, _43_, 653-668.

Black, D. _The Behavior of Law._ New York: Academic Press, 1976.

Bremner, R. H. _Children and Youth in America._ Cambridge: Harvard University Press, 1970.

Doyle, W. Are students behaving worse thay they used to behave? _Journal of Research and Development in Education_, 1978, _11_, 3-16.

Dugdale, R. _The Jukes: A Study in Crime, Pauperism, Disease, and Heredity._ New York: G.P. Putnam, 1877.

Erickson, E. _Identity: Youth and Crises._ New York: Norton, 1968.

Feldhusen, J. Behavior problems in secondary schools. _Journal of Research and Development in Education_, 1978, _11_, 17-28.

Higham, J. _Strangers in the Land._ New York: Atheneum, 1971.

Hofstader, R. Anti-intellectualism in American Life. New York: Knopf, 1963.

Kaestle, C. Social change, discipline, and the common school in early nineteenth century America. _The Journal of Interdisciplinary History_, 1978, _9_, 1-17.

Lorenz, K. The companion in the bird's world. _The Auk_, 1937, _54_, 245-273.

Piaget, J., & Inhelder, B. _The Psychology of the Child._ New York: Basic Books, 1969.

Platt, A. _The Child Savers._ Chicago: University of Chicago Press, 1977.

Robinson, N., & Robinson, H. _The Mentally Retarded Child._ New York: McGraw Hill, 1976.

References

Scott, J. & Marston, M. Critical periods affecting the development of normal and maladjustive social behavior of puppies. _Journal of Genetic Psychology_, 1950, _77_, 25-60.

Seaver, E. The care of truants and incorrigibles. _Educational Review_, 1894, _7_, 423-438.

Spencer, H. _Education: Intellectual, Moral and Physical_. New York: D. Appleton, 1896.

Thorndike, E. _Educational Psychology: The Original Nature of Man_ (Vol. 1), New York: Teachers College, Columbia University, 1913.

AUTHOR INDEX

Albert, M., 119, 129
Anderson, D., 121, 130
Andrews, R., 68, 82
Auerback, A., 48, 50
Bachara, G., 68, 82
Bachrach, H., 48, 50
Barchus, F., 70, 82
Gassioni, M., 85, 118, 129
Beady, C., 19, 29
Beck, R., 136, 152
Bergin, A., 22, 29
Black, D., 123, 129, 152
Blackstone, W., 107, 129
Blaney, P. H., 119, 129
Blauvelt, P., 47, 51, 62, 84
Bolmeier, E., 129
Bowdoin, G., 108, 129
Bowen, M., 9, 11, 36, 37, 50
Brannigan, G., 119, 129
Bremmer, R., 134, 152
Broden, M., 78, 82
Brookover, M., 19, 29
Brophy, J., 25, 29
Bryan, T., 68, 82
Buber, M., 79, 82, 102, 103, 106
Campbell, E., 118, 129
Chandler, M., 48, 50
Chawst, J., 119, 129
Children's Defense Fund, 112, 129
Coleman, J., 118, 129
Collins, G., 25, 30
Connor, C., 25, 31
Connors, E., 130
Cravens, R., 120, 129
Crutchfield, R., 25, 29
DeCecco, J., 8, 11, 19, 29
Di Giuseppe, R., 77, 82
Donnewerth, G., 119, 130
Doyle, W., 136, 152
Dugdale, R., 135, 152
Dyer, F., 3, 11
Elliot, D., 19, 29, 92, 106
Ellis, A., 76, 77, 82
Empey, L., 19, 29
Erickson, E., 19, 29
Erikson, E., 4, 11, 146, 152
Erikson, K. T., 27, 29
Evans, R. G., 119, 130

AUTHOR INDEX

AUTHOR INDEX

AUTHOR INDEX

Seaver, E., 135, 153
Sites, P., 27, 31
Skon, L., 26, 30
Spenser, H., 135, 153
Stephen, H., 123, 131
Stewart, M., 75, 83
Stone, A., 48, 50
Stone, B., 27, 31
Suzler, B., 84
Szasz, T., 78, 84
Teichman, M., 119, 130
Thorndike, E., 135, 153
Tittle, C., 17, 31
Turiel, E., 21, 30, 41, 50
Vestermark, S., 47, 51, 62, 84
Voss, H., 19, 29, 92, 106
Wallach, A., 27, 31
Wanty, 119, 130
Weinfeld, F., 119, 129
Whiddon, T., 28, 30
Wisenbacker, J., 19, 29
Worchel, P., 120, 129
York, R., 119, 129
Zechauser, R., 88, 106

SUBJECT INDEX

acceptable behavior, boundary change, 56-62, 133, 138-140

Amendments, First, 115
    Fourteenth, 109, 111
    Twenty-sixth, 109

analytical descriptions, effects of, 100

anger, and humiliation, 93, 94

attachment, to others, 14, 17

Baker, and due process, 113-114

basic needs, 14, 15

behavior modification, 53, 56, 72-78, 96, 137

boards of education, 1, 2, 4

Brown decision, 108, 109

child advocate model, 150-151

children, status of, 133-136, 147-149

ceremony, and ritual, 63-64

chaos, imposing order on, 56, 62-66

communion, 79, 80, 101-105

competition, 26, 27

compulsory attendance, 109

conformity, 13-28, 33, 34
    definitions of, 13
    dysfunctions of, 27-28
    functions of, 25-27
    influences to, 14-25

co-operation, 26, 27

corporatl punishment, 98, 113-114, 133

cost-benefit analysis, and justice, 88

SUBJECT INDEX

courtship model, 43

covert verbalizations, 56, 72-77

creativity, 4, 5, 80

critical periods, 146-147, 150

definition, of self, 10, 59, 60

delinquency, and surveillance, 92

depression, and social maladjustment, 119-120

deviance, 1-10
    definitions of, 2-3
    functions of, 4-9
    need for, 3-10, 33
    types of, 6

differences, acknowledging, respecting, 56, 78, 80

differentiation, of self, 5, 9, 17
    of groups, 27

diplomacy, 43

discipline, 1, 107, 111, 114, 116, 117, 118, 133-151

due process, and school discipline, 110-113

emotional sensitivity, development of, 126-127

English law, 107, 123

ethics, and morality, 126-127

equity theory, and perceptions of justice, 120-121

experts, and discipline, 136-137

expulsion, 113

frustration, and aggression, 98

gangs, 34-36. 39, 44, 46

Gault decision, and procedural due process, 110-112

SUBJECT INDEX

gifted, emotionally or morally, 125-128

groups, conforming, 33-34
    crystallized, 34
    deviant, 33-49
    disbanding of, 38
    fluid, 34
    formal, 36, 42, 44-47
    formation of, 33, 34, 38, 41, 42
    functions of, 33-49
    hanging, 36, 40, 42
    informal, 36-44
    interventions with, 36, 38-47
    organized, formal, 44-47
    reference, 2, 56, 72
    regressive group phenomenon, 41
    and stress, 35, 39
    structure of, 34, 35
    types of, 34-36, 98-99

groupthink, 45

handicapped, exceptional, 2, 8, 9, 54, 86, 94-95, 111, 125

holistic acceptance, of persons, 101-105

humiliation, and discipline, 93, 98

impression management, 15, 16, 101

individual rights and school discipline, 115-117

Ingraham vs. Wright, 113

in loco parentis and school discipline, 115-117

interdisciplinary model, 145

internal control, 44

interventions, with informal groups, 39-44
    with formal groups, 44-47
    with mobs, 47-49

justice, 48, 85-95, 118-122

SUBJECT INDEX

justice, perceptions of, 121, 122
    as fairness, 89, 92-95
    of parity, 121

Kent decision, and juvenile rights, 110

labels, 3

legal considerations, and discipline, 95, 96, 107-118

locus of control, 118, 119, 120

love, 5, 40, 127

Lopez, 111, 112

loyalty, 33, 34

majority, and rights of, 88, 89, 92

margin of safety, 57, 58

medical model, 144, 145

mobs, 47-49

moral development, stages of, 21, 22, 118
    and groups, use of, 41
    and training for, 126, 127

multi-cultural programs, 15

norms, laws, unwritten, 138-139, 152

narrowing boundaries, acceptable behavior, 56-62, 133,
    138-140

organizations, 36, 39

parity, as justice, 121

passivity, 14, 23, 25

peer recognition, 43

pregnancy, of teenagers, 119

Plessy vs. Ferguson, 108, 109

SUBJECT INDEX

power, 122, 123

punishment, 33, 116, 122, 123
    corporatl, 98, 113-114, 133

Public Law 94-142, 111, 137, 142

Reality Therapy, 41

recognition, and awards for achievement, 94, 97, 121,
    124

recognition, of the individual, 133

recognition, peer, 43

reference groups, 2

regressive group phenomenon, 41

role taking, and information, 56, 68-72

rumors, 47, 48

school climate, 19, 20, 55

school, as duty, 97, 98
    as government, 98, 99
    as holistic acceptance, 100-105
    as inquiry, 99, 100
    as privilege, 96, 97

segregation, effects of, 9

self-actualization, and fairness, 88

self-esteem, 14, 22, 23

self-identity, and expectations of justice, 91

self-respect, 40, 89, 90, 93, 94

socially acceptable, envelopment in, 14 18-21

social conditions, and discipline, 96, 100, 107-108

social expectations, core, 133

163

SUBJECT INDEX

social needs, 14-18

suspension, internal, 93

suspension, short term vs. long term, 111-113

tension, lowering, of 56, 66-68

<u>Tinker</u> decision, free speech and discipline, 114-115

typology, for discipline, 53, 55, 56

utilitarian ethics, 88, 91

visibility of violation, 57

victims, and comfort of others, 85-87

wisdom, development of, 100

ABOUT THE AUTHOR

Eve E. Gagne has been an educator for the past eighteen years. While at Saint Joseph's College she studied English literature and sociology; she later obtained a Master's degree in education from the University of Hartford and a Ph.D. from the University of Connecticut. Dr. Gagne has taught in regular public elementary and high schools, special schools for the behaviorally disordered, and in state institutions. She has been a faculty member at the State University of New York at Binghamton and she is currently an associate professor of special education at Chicago State University. She has published articles in the field of delinquency, as well as in other areas of special education, and she has done consulting work in the areas of school discipline and delinquency. Dr. Gagne is presently teaching courses in school discipline at Chicago State University.

Dr. Gagne has visited, and worked in schools in the northeastern, western, southern, and midwestern parts of the United States and she has visited schools in the Scandinavian countries and in the Soviet Union. Dr. Gagne's current concern is what she perceives to be an overemphasis on analytical approaches in dealing with people and a neglect of holistic acceptance, which she feels represents a serious problem at both the personal and societal levels. Holistic acceptance of persons, in place of the use of analytical considerations, would result in a decrease in the use of labels, improvements in inter-personal communication, greater concern for the human condition, and deepened concern for others.

Dr. Gagne's plans for the future include consulting activities regarding a systems approach to school discipline, and in the area of juvenile delinquency. She also plans to develop multi-media materials in the area of holistic acceptance of others for both teachers and students.

165

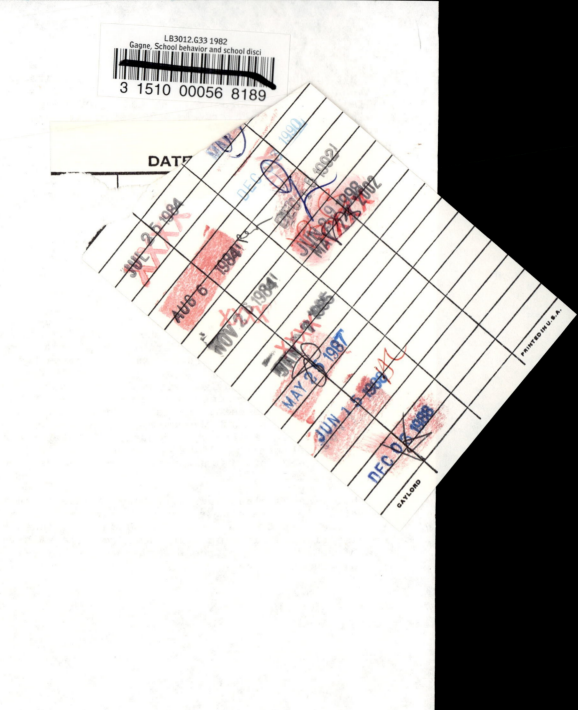